ELIZABETH M............Y

2014

A BOOK OF
GRACE-FILLED
DAYS

LOYOLA PRESS.
A JESUIT MINISTRY

Chicago

LOYOLA PRESS.
A JESUIT MINISTRY

3441 N. Ashland Avenue
Chicago, Illinois 60657
(800) 621-1008
www.loyolapress.com

Cover and interior design by Kathy Kikkert.

ISBN-13: 978-0-8294-3626-6
ISBN-10: 0-8294-3626-X
Library of Congress Control Number: 2013936209

Printed in the United States of America.

13 14 15 16 17 18 Bang 10 9 8 7 6 5 4 3 2 1

INTRODUCTION

In 2011, pope emeritus Benedict XVI delivered a series of general audiences he referred to as "a school of prayer."[1] Highlighting the notion that "Prayer is . . . written on the heart of every person and of every civilization," the Holy Father examined meditation, silence, spiritual reading, intercession, and other elements necessary to a thriving life of prayer. "Each one of us needs time and space for recollection, meditation, and calmness," he said. "Thanks be to God that this is so! In fact, this need tells us that we are not made for work alone, but also to think, to reflect or even simply to follow with our minds and our hearts a tale, a story in which to immerse ourselves, in a certain sense 'to lose ourselves' to find ourselves subsequently enriched."

Indeed, this is the goal of our time spent together here in these pages—to lose ourselves in order to find ourselves enriched by God's presence. Or perhaps even more

---

1. These are all available on the Vatican website beginning with the General Audience in St. Peter's Square on May 4, 2011.

accurately, to lose ourselves that Jesus might find us and invite us into his eternal story.

Your story, my story, our life's tale is written into every page of Holy Scripture. We are there with Joseph and Mary and Herod, with angels and kings, slaves and prophets, Magdalenes, Prodigals, and good thieves, living out a common life. This is an eternal narrative flowing through the rhythms of the liturgical seasons and the seasons of human life—one that cannot be separated out by time, culture, socioeconomic status, sex, or race, one that will not be quashed by death. The challenge the ancient Israelites faced, of living holy, virtuous lives, is our challenge, too. Whether we see the Good Samaritan or Peter filled with fear, the murder of the Holy Innocents or David striking down Goliath, these accounts reflect not only the individual struggle for holiness but the whole Church's struggle to grow in virtue and to live out the truth. In our failures and in our successes, we are accountable, but we are not alone.

We meet one another here in this time of prayer and meditation, to address a universal need deeply embedded in the human person. "Prayer is centred and rooted in the inmost depths of the person," said pope emeritus Benedict XVI. "The philosopher Ludwig Wittgenstein mentioned that 'prayer means feeling that the world's meaning is outside the world.'" Prayer and meditation with the Word of God opens us to live and love this wonderful paradox: in our deepest selves we sense meaning *beyond* ourselves. We understand ourselves to be part of a much more sweeping narrative than the year 2014, but instead a part of eternity. We step into these tiny pages and passages to step out of ourselves and our own littleness and into the greatness of God's vast, delightful, eternal plan.

We might be tempted to rush through these readings because they are fairly short and the pages are small. But I would leave you with some practical advice offered by the Holy Father, which echoes the help we can find from Mary and the saints who have come before us in this school of prayer:

> Mary teaches us how necessary it is to find in our busy day, moments for silent recollection, to meditate on what the Lord wants to teach us, on how he is present and active in the world and in our life: to be able to stop for a moment and meditate . . . "to ruminate"; that is the mysteries of God should continually resonate within us so that they become familiar to us, guide our lives and nourish us, as does the food we need to sustain us. . . . To meditate, therefore, means to create within us a situation of recollection, of inner silence, in

order to reflect upon and assimilate the mysteries of our faith and what God is working within us; and not merely on the things that come and go.

We take a deep breath, we read slowly, and again. We sit and ruminate and find refreshment. We allow heart and mind to settle on the word God wishes to give us, we practice receiving and accepting, and we find rest, peace, a moment of stillness, and union with the Lord God, Jehovah. Thus fortified, we can return to the day.

Pope emeritus Benedict XVI noted that "Man bears within him a thirst for the infinite, a longing for eternity, a quest for beauty, a desire for love, a need for light and for truth which impel him towards the Absolute; man bears within him the desire for God. And man knows, in a certain way, that he can turn to God, he knows he can pray to him."

You know, *you can pray to Him*.

Immerse yourself in this grand adventure. Follow with your mind and your heart this story, your story, our story. May you lose yourself and find yourself in the eternal telling and retelling of our saving Jesus Christ.

The night is advanced, the day is at hand. Let us then throw off
the works of darkness and put on the armor of light.
—ROMANS 13:12

The sun of salvation rises; Advent announces the dawn on
which all the promises of love are fulfilled. This is love that
is credible and durable, a love that will not fail.

Isaiah 2:1–5
Psalm 122
Romans 13:11–14
Matthew 24:37–44

⋟ 1 ⋞

DECEMBER 2

*May peace be within your walls,
prosperity in your buildings . . .*

*I will say, "Peace be within you!"
Because of the house of the LORD, our God,
I will pray for your good.*
—PSALM 122:7–9

David and his dad were in an accident; David survived but
his father did not. David had to have multiple surgeries
afterward, and every time he came out of anesthesia, he
woke up remembering the crash and yelling, "Dad, please
don't be dead!" But one day David's grandparents prayed
while sitting in Adoration: "We offer this hour for our
grandson. In this next surgery, may he wake up singing and
laughing." And singing and laughing, he did.

Lord, who needs my prayers for good today?

Isaiah 4:2–6
Psalm 122
Matthew 8:5–11

⇛ 2 ⇚

DECEMBER 3

• ST. FRANCIS XAVIER, PRIEST •

With a little child to guide them.
—ISAIAH 11:6

Power and wisdom and might are not always found where we
might first look for them, and they don't always work the
way we imagine. Heaven is filled with paradoxes that
increase our humility. Holiness is what makes us powerful.
Virtue gives us wisdom and might. Love is the only lasting
power there is.

Isaiah 11:1–10
Psalm 72
Luke 10:21–24

Wednesday

DECEMBER 4

• ST. JOHN DAMASCENE, PRIEST AND DOCTOR OF THE CHURCH •

He guides me in right paths
for his name's sake.
Even though I walk in the dark valley
I fear no evil; for you are at my side
With your rod and your staff
that give me courage.
—PSALM 23:3–4

Courage, little one, he is with you.

Isaiah 25:6–10a
Psalm 23
Matthew 15:29–37

DECEMBER 5

"Everyone who listens to these words of mine and acts on them will be like a wise man who built his house on rock."
—MATTHEW 7:24

Listen and act: the formula is quite simple. Do I do both, and in that order?

Isaiah 26:1–6
Psalm 118
Matthew 7:21, 24–27

And their eyes were opened.
—MATTHEW 9:30

This is always the work of Jesus—to bring me out of darkness and into the light. He has no interest in abandoning me to my own sin and spiritual squalor. He is not interested in bringing me into the gray or half-measures. The restoration he offers is complete and full. The question is, am I willing to really see that well?

Isaiah 29:17–24
Psalm 27
Matthew 9:27–31

DECEMBER 7

• ST. AMBROSE, BISHOP AND DOCTOR OF THE CHURCH •

*Then he summoned his Twelve disciples and gave them
authority over unclean spirits to drive them out and to cure
every disease and every illness.*
—MATTHEW 10:1

For all his wisdom and intellectual acumen, St. Ambrose had
a very practical side. "We believe fishermen," he says, "not
dialecticians." Study is important and prayer is absolutely
necessary, but above all we are given the graces necessary to
do the work God has assigned to our lives. We believe he
gives grace out of his great love and mercy, not because we
somehow have earned it.

Isaiah 30:19–21, 23–26
Psalm 147
Matthew 9:35—10:1, 5a, 6–8

DECEMBER 8

• SECOND SUNDAY OF ADVENT •

By endurance and by the encouragement of the Scriptures we might have hope.
—ROMANS 15:4

Despair and presumption are considered the two sins against hope. As our *Catechism* notes, "Despair is contrary to God's goodness . . . for the Lord is faithful to his promises—and to his mercy." But neither can we presume to save ourselves or obtain forgiveness without true contrition. Hope is not situated in the world of men but in the divine heart of God. It is not won easily. But through endurance and our engagement of God's word and works, we grow in its direction.

Isaiah 11:1–10
Psalm 72
Romans 15:4–9
Matthew 3:1–12

DECEMBER 9

• IMMACULATE CONCEPTION OF THE BLESSED VIRGIN MARY •

Mary said, "Behold, I am the handmaid of the Lord. May it be done to me according to your word."
—LUKE 1:38

Have you ever been tempted to imagine that Mary was simply capricious or reckless, naïve? "So completely have we depended upon material things," writes Caryll Houselander, "on money in particular, so terribly are we influenced by fear that simply to abandon ourselves to God and really to mean it seems to be madness."

This Advent, may we all go a little crazy—abandoning our lives to Christ. Jesus, do with me as you wish.

Genesis 3:9–15, 20
Psalm 98
Ephesians 1:3–6, 11–12
Luke 1:26–38

DECEMBER 10

Though the grass withers and the flower wilts,
the word of our God stands forever.
—ISAIAH 40:8

Today, I place myself in the reality of eternity. As pope emeritus Benedict XVI exhorts us, "Here on earth, we are called to look up to heaven, to turn our minds and hearts to the inexpressible mystery of God. We are called to look towards this divine reality, to which we have been directed from our creation. For there we find life's ultimate meaning."

Isaiah 40:1–11
Psalm 96
Matthew 18:12–14

"Take my yoke upon you and learn from me, for I am meek and humble of heart; and you will find rest for yourselves."
—MATTHEW 11:29

Meekness has fallen out of fashion. Instead we take assertiveness training courses. We barely recognize true humility and when we see it, we treat it with suspicion or disdain. Wouldn't it be wonderful to put down all the pretense, all the effort of trying to do something and be someone in the world—and instead take up the yoke of Christ? Wouldn't it be a relief to be who you are? The rest comes not because you stop working, but because you stop working to be something you aren't and instead allow Christ to lead you into authenticity.

Isaiah 40:25–31
Psalm 103
Matthew 11:28–30

Thursday

DECEMBER 12

• OUR LADY OF GUADALUPE •

Many nations shall join themselves to the LORD on that day,
and they shall be his people, and he will dwell among you.
—ZECHARIAH 2:15

We invoke your intercession, Blessed Mother, Our Lady of
Guadalupe. You appear to us in ways we can understand. We
pray for all our Catholic Christian brethren who suffer
religious persecution for their faith. We ask you to cover
them in your mantle, give them courage of heart and firm
faith in the presence of your Son in their suffering.

Zechariah 2:14–17 or Revelation
11:19a; 12:1–6a, 10ab
Judith 13:18bcde, 19
Luke 1:26–38 or 1:39–47

I, the LORD, your God,
teach you what is for your good,
and lead you on the way you should go.
—ISAIAH 48:17

A friend was overwhelmed by difficult circumstances—an alcoholic husband who refused help along with the financial and social strain that accompanies such a situation. "I don't know what to do," she cried to her priest. "But he does," the priest replied. "We don't see it yet, but God has a way." And he did. Day by day, step by step, she was led. And she found that God's great goodness attended and steadied her along the way.

Isaiah 48:17–19
Psalm 1
Matthew 11:16–19

Saturday

DECEMBER 14

• ST. JOHN OF THE CROSS, PRIEST AND DOCTOR OF THE CHURCH •

"So also will the Son of Man suffer at their hands."
—MATTHEW 17:12

We might be tempted to cower here and rescind our hearts at the promise of suffering. John of the Cross wrote, "See that you are not suddenly saddened by the adversities of this world, for you do not know the good they bring, being ordained in the judgments of God for the everlasting joy of the elect." In other words, eternal life and salvation for all.

St. John of the Cross, pray for us.

Sirach 48:1–4, 9–11
Psalm 80
Matthew 17: 9a, 10–13

⇒ 14 ⇐

Sunday

DECEMBER 15

• THIRD SUNDAY OF ADVENT •

Say to those whose hearts are frightened:
Be strong, fear not!
—ISAIAH 35:4

Can you offer to God the thing that scares you the most?
Can you place it in his hands and leave it there, just for the
day, and see what happens? Can you get up tomorrow and
do the same thing?

Isaiah 35:1–6a, 10
Psalm 146
James 5:7–10
Matthew 11:2–11

⇒ 15 ⇐

DECEMBER 16

Remember that your compassion, O LORD,
and your kindness are from of old.
In your kindness remember me,
because of your goodness, O LORD.
—PSALM 25:6–7

Does God need reminding of his goodness, compassion, and
kindness—or do I?

Lord, I trust in you; you do not forget me or abandon me.

Numbers 24:2–7, 15–17a
Psalm 25
Matthew 21:23–27

DECEMBER 17

Of her was born Jesus who is called the Christ.
—MATTHEW 1:16

The poetry of John of the Cross beckons:

The Virgin, weighed
with the word of God
comes down the road
if only you'll shelter her.

May Jesus find shelter in me. Pray for us, O Holy Mother
of God.

Genesis 49:2, 8–10
Psalm 72
Matthew 1:1–17

—

Joseph her husband, since he was a righteous man, yet unwilling to expose her to shame, decided to divorce her quietly.
—MATTHEW 1:19

For all the glory of anticipating Virgin Mother and Child, we might take a moment to remember Joseph's role in the Incarnation. In *Redemptoris Custos*, Blessed John Paul II wrote, "Together with Mary, Joseph is the first guardian of this divine mystery. Together with Mary and in relation to Mary, he shares in this final phase of God's self-revelation in Christ and he does so from the very beginning. . . . Through God's mysterious design, it was in that family that the Son of God spent long years of a hidden life."

Jeremiah 23:5–8
Psalm 72
Matthew 1:18–25

DECEMBER 19

*The angel of the Lord appeared to him, standing at the right of
the altar of incense. Zechariah was troubled by what he saw,
and fear came upon him.*
—LUKE 1:11–12

We are quick to imagine angels as benign, gentle beings, and
yet Scripture is clear to note that their presence often
invoked fear, confusion, and terror. I do not wish you terror
for Christmas, of course; what I hope for you is a renewed
sense of the awesome and terrible power of God.
Considering God's choice then to come to us in the form of a
vulnerable, helpless child, we pay even closer attention to
what that might mean.

Judges 13:2–7, 24–25a
Psalm 71
Luke 1:5–25

The Lord himself will give you this sign; the virgin shall conceive and bear a son, and shall name him Emmanuel.
—ISAIAH 7:14

We ask for signs all the time. *Lord, give me a sign, so I know what to do.*

I once told a spiritual director that I needed a real friend, a true friend, who could help keep me accountable and on the straight and narrow. He pointed to the crucifix and said, "You have one." I'd say the same here. You want signs? You have one: Emmanuel, God with us.

Isaiah 7:10–14
Psalm 24
Luke 1:26–38

Arise, my beloved, my beautiful one,
and come!
—SONG OF SONGS 2:10

John of the Cross gave the Church some of the most moving mystical poetry ever written. Hear these verses (translated by Kieran Kavanaugh) as from the Beloved.

When you looked at me
your eyes imprinted your grace in me;
for this you loved me ardently;
and thus my eyes deserved
to adore what they beheld in you . . .
now truly you can look at me
since you have looked
and left in me grace and beauty.

Song of Songs 2:8–14 or
Zephaniah 3:14–18a
Psalm 33
Luke 1:39–45

⇒ 21 ⇐

DECEMBER 22

• FOURTH SUNDAY OF ADVENT •

Through him we have received the grace of apostleship, to bring about the obedience of faith, for the sake of his name . . . who are called to belong to Jesus Christ; to all the beloved of God in Rome, called to be holy.
—ROMANS 1:5–7

Are you wondering about your vocation—what God is asking you to do in this day, how to address a particular problem or difficulty? Are you wondering how you might thank him for this season of Advent, overflowing with graces and every blessing?

Beloved, you who belong to Jesus, be holy.

Isaiah 7:10–14
Psalm 24
Romans 1:1–7
Matthew 1:18–24

"John is his name."
—LUKE 1:63

Joseph Cardinal Ratzinger wrote in *Jesus of Nazareth*: "These ancients words of hope were brought into the present with the Baptist's preaching: Great things are about to unfold. We can imagine the extraordinary impression that the figure and message of John the Baptist must have produced in the highly charged atmosphere of Jerusalem at that particular moment of history. At last there was a prophet again, and his life marked him out as such. God's hand was at last plainly acting in history again. John baptizes with water, but one even greater, who will baptize with the Holy Spirit and fire, is already at the door."

Malachi 3:1–4, 23–24
Psalm 25
Luke 1:57–66

DECEMBER 24

You, my child, shall be called the prophet of the Most High,
for you will go before the Lord to prepare his way,
to give his people knowledge of salvation
by the forgiveness of their sins.
—LUKE 1:76–77

Zechariah's prophesy celebrates John the Baptist and all that
would be accomplished by his ministry through the grace of
God. Today we remember the parents of all men and women
who choose to serve the Church with their whole lives as
priests, religious, or consecrated. May their vocations be
supported and celebrated by those who love them most.

2 Samuel 7:1–5, 8b–12, 14a, 16
Psalm 89
Luke 1:67–79

Wednesday

DECEMBER 25

• THE NATIVITY OF THE LORD—CHRISTMAS •

And Mary kept all these things, reflecting on them in her heart.
—LUKE 2:19

Amidst the joy and feasting, the decorating and sharing of
gifts, the hubbub and family visits—in whatever way we
might celebrate Christmas—we find time today to draw
away for a while. In quiet contemplation we join Mary most
holy, in reflection and deep thanksgiving.

VIGIL:
Isaiah 62:1–5
Psalm 89
Acts 13:16–17, 22–25
Matthew 1:1–25 or 1:18–25

MIDNIGHT:
Isaiah 9:1–6
Psalm 96
Titus 2:11–14
Luke 2:1–14

DAWN:
Isaiah 62:11–12
Psalm 97
Titus 3:4–7
Luke 2:15–20

DAY:
Isaiah 52:7–10
Psalm 98
Hebrews 1:1–6
John 1:1–18 or 1:1–5, 9–14

DECEMBER 26

• ST. STEPHEN, FIRST MARTYR •

*When they heard this, they were infuriated, and they ground
their teeth at him. But [Stephen], filled with the Holy Spirit,
looked up intently to heaven and saw the glory of God and
Jesus . . . and he said, "Behold, I see the heavens opened and the
Son of Man . . ." But they cried out in a loud voice, covered
their ears and rushed upon him together.*
—ACTS 7:54–57

A friend receives hate mail and threatening phone calls when
she defends marriage in the public square. We are not
surprised when met with outright hatred and persecution for
living by and teaching the truths of our faith: life begins at
conception; all have a right to life and a natural death, no
matter their capacities; capital punishment is wrong; sex
outside of marriage diminishes sex within marriage; marriage
between a man and a woman is sacrosanct. Sin is real—and
so is absolution.

Acts 6:8–10; 7:54–59
Psalm 31
Matthew 10:17–22

Then the other disciple also went in, the one who had arrived at the tomb first, and he saw and believed.
—JOHN 20:8

What curious details to include in the Gospel—that John should run faster than Peter, that he should arrive first yet allow Peter to enter the tomb before him.

There is supernatural order to all things. And one who is open to the subtle moves of the Spirit is in step with heaven's eternal plan right down to the smallest detail.

1 John 1:1–4
Psalm 97
John 20:1a, 2–8

He ordered the massacre of all the boys in Bethlehem . . .
"A voice was heard in Ramah,
sobbing and loud lamentation;
Rachel weeping for her children,
and she would not be consoled,
since they were no more."
—MATTHEW 2:16, 18

Holy innocents are still being massacred. Are we weeping?

We pray for the unborn and those who work to protect them; we pray for young mothers and fathers, poor mothers and fathers, single parents, and any struggling to raise their children to love and serve the Lord.

1 John 1:5—2:2
Psalm 124
Matthew 2:13–18

Take care of your father when he is old;
grieve him not as long as he lives.
—SIRACH 3:12

Sherry Turkle's troubling book, *Alone Together: Why We Expect More from Technology and Less from Each Other,* outlines the development of sociable robots, some designed to take care of the elderly and "keep them company." "The very fact that we now design and manufacture robot companions for the elderly marks a turning point," says Turkle. "We ask technology to perform what used to be 'love's labor': taking care of each other." As one small child remarked, "Why don't we have people for these jobs?"

What does it mean to be "a holy family"?

Sirach 3:2–6, 12–14
Psalm 128
Colossians 3:12–21 or 3:12–17
Matthew 2:13–15, 19–23

Monday

DECEMBER 30

*I write to you young men, because you are strong and the word
of God remains in you, and you have conquered the Evil One.*
—1 JOHN 2:14

John ticks off his addressees: children, fathers, young men.
We can surely include young women in this list. Are we
raising our young people to be strong, filling them with the
Word of God so that they are prepared to enter the wider
world and do good, to live heroically holy lives?

1 John 2:12–17
Psalm 96
Luke 2:36–40

Tuesday

DECEMBER 31

• ST. SYLVESTER I, POPE •

All things came to be through him,
and without him nothing came to be.
What came to be through him was life,
and this life was the light of the human race;
the light shines in the darkness,
and the darkness has not overcome it.
—JOHN 1:3–5

May all things come to be in this New Year through him, the light of the human race. This year, Lord, may I be a light that the darkness cannot overcome.

Happy New Year.

1 John 2:18–21
Psalm 96
John 1:1–18

Wednesday

JANUARY 1

• SOLEMNITY OF MARY, MOTHER OF GOD •

*When the fullness of time had come, God sent his Son, born of
a woman . . . to ransom those under the law, so that we might
receive adoption as sons.*
—GALATIANS 4:4–5

Saint Thomas Aquinas said that "grace perfects nature." That
God should choose to come into our midst through such a
natural event, that he would be born into our world, born of
a woman, that he would free us through a blood-born
relationship—all this tells us how very natural, critically
important, and perfectible family life is. The relationships
established within the family become grace—when they are
ordered toward heaven.

Numbers 6:22–27
Psalm 67
Galatians 4:4–7
Luke 2:16–21

Thursday

JANUARY 2

• ST. BASIL THE GREAT AND ST. GREGORY NAZIANZEN, BISHOPS AND DOCTORS OF THE CHURCH •

This is the promise that he made us: eternal life.
—1 JOHN 2:25

Heaven is not the escape hatch for all of life's problems; heaven is the promise that God will live with us forever in a way we cannot imagine. Like the baby still in the womb awaiting birth into the wider, very real world, so do we prepare for the promise of Christ: eternal life.

1 John 2:22–28
Psalm 98
John 1:19–28

"'He is the one who will baptize with the Holy Spirit.'"
—JOHN 1:33

It is entirely human to be filled with doubt sometimes, but we can rest in the clarity of the Word of God. Scripture is completely plain: Jesus is the one who has come to save us, redeem and anoint us, to welcome us into eternity.

Lord, all the answers to all my questions rest in You, the One.

1 John 2:29—3:6
Psalm 98
John 1:29–34

Saturday

JANUARY 4

• ST. ELIZABETH ANN SETON, RELIGIOUS •

Let the sea and what fills it resound,
the world and those who dwell in it;
Let the rivers clap their hands,
the mountains shout with them for joy before the LORD.
The LORD comes;
he comes to rule the earth;
He will rule the world with justice
and the peoples with equity.
—PSALM 98:7–9

Today, can I celebrate the mighty grandeur of the Lord God?
Whether in my cubicle, on the subway, in my car, dressing
my children, or solving a complex problem with a client, I
will remember: the rivers clap, the mountains shout for joy.
He comes. He comes to rule with justice.

1 John 3:7–10
Psalm 98
John 1:35–42

Rise up in splendor, Jerusalem! Your light has come,
the glory of the Lord shines upon you.
—ISAIAH 60:1

"And behold, the star that [the magi] had seen at its rising
preceded them, until it came and stopped over the place
where the child was." God still uses light to draw us to him,
to help us find our way, to lead us through the night to
secret, holy places and the company of every possible saving
grace. He uses the light of the sacraments and prayer, the
light of his word, and the light in you.

Isaiah 60:1–6
Psalm 72
Ephesians 3:2–3a, 5–6
Matthew 2:1–12

The one who is in you is greater than the one who is in the world.
—1 JOHN 4:4

Do I believe it? Does my life look like the life of someone who understands, deep in her bones, that the God who dwells in me created and rules the world?

Lord, just for today, I will not cower in the face of the enemy. I will stand aright and trust in your greatness and mercy.

1 John 3:22—4:6
Psalm 2
Matthew 4:12–17, 23–25

Tuesday

JANUARY 7

• ST. RAYMOND OF PENYAFORT, PRIEST •

*He shall defend the afflicted among the people,
save the children of the poor.*
—PSALM 72:4

Through you and through me—this is how God defends the
afflicted and protects the innocent, feeds the hungry and
loves the lost. Blessed Mother Teresa said it this way: "Let us
touch the dying, the poor, the lonely and the unwanted
according to the graces we have received." God will do
the rest.

1 John 4:7–10
Psalm 72
Mark 6:34–44

JANUARY 8

On the contrary, their hearts were hardened.
—MARK 6:52

In the presence of miracles—loaves and fishes and healings—the apostles found themselves confused and disbelieving. How human! At times when I find myself stumbling in this way, a mentor tells me, "Welcome to the human race."

Jesus loves us so. He chose us. He loves us and chooses us still, even when our hearts are confounded and closed. Jesus, your love will outlive my confusion and hardness of heart. Only be patient with me awhile more.

1 John 4:11–18
Psalm 72
Mark 6:45–52

JANUARY 9

. . . he first loved us.
—1 JOHN 4:19

The original impulse always moves in our direction. We may
rest in knowing that God never gets stuck, is never static,
never falters, rescinds, nor retreats. He cannot fail to love us;
it's simply not possible.

1 John 4:19—5:4
Psalm 72
Luke 4:14–22a

JANUARY 10

The spirit, the water, and the Blood, and the three are of one accord.
—1 JOHN 5:8

We might think of it this way. Water represents Christ's baptism and his taking on our full humanity; blood is his passion and death; spirit is that which makes possible his resurrection. Not one of these may be removed from the others. Without humanity, Christ remains only divine; without his suffering, we have no means to redemption; without the spirit, we have no way to understand or enter the mystery of resurrection.

1 John 5:5–13
Psalm 147
Luke 5:12–16

JANUARY 11

*Beloved: We have this confidence in him that if we ask anything
according to his will, he hears us. And if we know that he hears
us in regard to whatever we ask, we know that what we have
asked him for is ours.*
—1 JOHN 5:14–15

My first prayer partner taught me a simple phrase that has
stayed with me: "Lord, if it be your perfect will . . ." She used
it to frame every request we launched toward heaven, and it
built in her precisely this confidence of which John writes.
Every prayer is heard—and answered—according to the
perfect will of God. I pray more and more, not for specific
answers, but that my heart will be aligned with the perfect
will of the Father.

1 John 5:14–21
Psalm 149
John 3:22–30

Here is my servant whom I uphold,
my chosen one with whom I am pleased,
upon whom I have put my spirit.
—ISAIAH 42:1

The Old Testament reaches forward into the New, ever
reminding us that truth exists outside of time. The temporal
serves the eternal in some way we cannot comprehend, but
the prophetic announcement of Jesus' baptism in Isaiah
confirms for us that we must set our hearts not on this world,
but on eternity. That is the territory and the "time" we are
truly meant to inhabit.

Isaiah 42:1–4, 6–7
Psalm 29
Acts 10:34–38
Matthew 3:13–17

My vows to the LORD I will pay
in the presence of all his people.
—PSALM 116:18

Vocation is a very public thing. We do not belong only to ourselves but to the whole Body of Christ. When we uphold our vows—to love, honor, and cherish; to poverty, chastity, and obedience; to love God and reject Satan; to proclaim Christ to the world—it's not simply a private matter. In our fidelity, we uphold one another.

1 Samuel 1:1–8
Psalm 116
Mark 1:14–20

"I was only pouring out my troubles to the LORD."
—1 SAMUEL 1:15

Hannah, bereft and long-tormented at her barren state, went and wept bitter, copious tears before the Lord. Don't think you were the first!

And in God's mercy, he answered her and she bore a son. He will answer us, too, in his mercy.

1 Samuel 1:9–20
1 Samuel 2:1, 4–5, 6–7, 8abcd
Mark 1:21–28

JANUARY 15

"Speak, LORD, for your servant is listening."
—1 SAMUEL 3:10

A student from Cuba taught me her country's proverb: "Listening looks easy, but it's not simple. Every head is a world." Indeed. It was the capacity to listen that placed Samuel firmly in the presence of the Lord, where no word was "without effect."

How often do I sit in silence before the Lord? Do I make it a habit to practice the prayer of quiet, to listen, to truly pay attention when I pray, to listen for the holy, mysterious voice of God?

1 Samuel 3:1–10, 19–20
Psalm 40
Mark 1:29–39

Why do you hide your face,
forgetting our woe and our oppression?
For our souls are bowed down to the dust,
our bodies are pressed to the earth.
—PSALM 44:25–26

The face of the Lord is most often revealed to us in one another. The Lord's face is hidden when we fail to attend to those who need us: the poor, the oppressed, the innocent and vulnerable, the mentally ill, the unborn, the aging, the lost, those cast off by society for being weird or different or difficult.

Lord, let your face shine through mine today. Through my attentiveness and care, lift my sisters and brothers from the dust and despair of their anguish.

1 Samuel 4:1–11
Psalm 44
Mark 1:40–45

Friday

JANUARY 17

• ST. ANTHONY, ABBOT •

When Jesus saw their faith, he said to him, "Child, your sins are forgiven."
—MARK 2:5

Only Jesus has the power to forgive sins, but we have the power to forgive one another. Sometimes, all forgiveness requires is a little faith in the one who needs forgiveness, or in the one who needs to forgive. Asking for forgiveness is in itself an act of faith; it's placing our trust in another's ability and desire to reconcile. Jesus responds to such faith and trust. Today may we build faith and trust into our relationships.

1 Samuel 8:4–7, 10–22a
Psalm 89
Mark 2:1–12

JANUARY 18

O LORD, in your strength the king is glad;
in your victory how greatly he rejoices!
You have granted him his heart's desire;
you refused not the wish of his lips.
—PSALM 21:2–3

A newly ordained priest I know glows in the dark! In his first years as a priest, I watched as his confidence grew. He positively beamed. But it was more than self-generated confidence; it was a holy confidence instilled by God through the ordination of a man well-prepared, chosen, and called to the priesthood. When we move in the confidence of God's call—the vocation for which we are called, chosen, and prepared—we beam with heaven's luminous, irresistible joy.

1 Samuel 9:1–4, 17–19; 10:1a
Psalm 21
Mark 2:13–17

Sunday

JANUARY 19

I will make you a light to the nations,
that my salvation may reach to the ends of the earth.
—ISAIAH 49:6

G. K. Chesterton said it this way: "Christianity is centrifugal: it breaks out. . . . [T]he cross, though it has at its heart a collision and a contradiction, can extend its four arms for ever without altering its shape. Because it has paradox in its centre it can grow without changing. . . . The cross opens its arms to the four winds; it is a signpost for free travellers." A light to the nations.

Isaiah 49:3, 5–6
Psalm 40
1 Corinthians 1:1–3
John 1:29–34

Obedience is better than sacrifice,
and submission than the fat of rams.
For a sin like divination is rebellion,
and presumption is the crime of idolatry.
—1 SAMUEL 15:22–23

Sacrifice might come from my pocketbook or my pantry, but obedience must spring from the heart and will. Presumption and rebellion can grow up only in a heart willful and maligned.

Lord, let me see submission to your will as it truly is—not a mindless, pathetic cowering, but a loving, necessary alignment of my heart to the plan of heaven and the reality of your sovereignty.

1 Samuel 15:16–23
Psalm 50
Mark 2:18–22

Tuesday

JANUARY 21

• ST. AGNES, VIRGIN AND MARTYR •

*"The sabbath was made for man, not man for the sabbath. That
is why the Son of Man is lord even of the sabbath."*
—MARK 2:27–28

We're given sabbath for resting and setting aright our spirit.
It is a gift of remembrance of God's goodness that protects
and restores us. Indeed, all the work of the Son of Man is to
protect us and restore us to him.

Does my Sunday look like a day of restoration to and
remembrance of the Lord?

1 Samuel 16:1–13
Psalm 89
Mark 2:23–28

JANUARY 22

Looking around at them with anger and grieved at their hardness of heart, Jesus said to the man, "Stretch out your hand." He stretched it out and his hand was restored.
—MARK 3:5

Angry and grieving, Jesus, as always, is driven to heal, to do the will of the Father. This is an important lesson when we experience difficult emotions. No matter what we might be feeling, we can follow Jesus in this, looking for ways to bring healing and heaven's grace to every painful, uncomfortable situation.

1 Samuel 17:32–33, 37, 40–51
Psalm 144
Mark 3:1–6

• ST. VINCENT, DEACON AND MARTYR •

My wanderings you have counted;
my tears are stored in your flask.
—PSALM 56:9

In the *Dialogues*, Jesus tells Catherine of Siena that "every tear proceeds from the heart, for there is no member of the body that will satisfy the heart so much as the eye. If the heart is in pain the eye manifests it."

Lord, give me eyes to see the tears of the world, to pray for the suffering of others, to value and see my own suffering as you do—stored up so that one day it should be used to quench the sorrowful thirst of another.

1 Samuel 18:6–9; 19:1–7
Psalm 56
Mark 3:7–12

Friday

JANUARY 24

*Saul then said to David ". . . you have treated me generously,
while I had done you harm. Great is the generosity you showed
me today, when the LORD delivered me into your grasp and you
did not kill me."*
—1 SAMUEL 24:18–19

The human heart's natural inclination is to exact revenge
when it has been wounded. But this is not God's way. Again
and again he shows us his mercy throughout Scripture. It is
good to be reminded, as St. Francis de Sales says, "Nothing is
so strong as gentleness, nothing so gentle as real strength."

Jesus, make me gentle and strong.

1 Samuel 24:3–21
Psalm 57
Mark 3:13–19

So Ananias went and entered the house; laying his hands on him, he said, "Saul, my brother, the Lord has sent me, Jesus who appeared to you on the way by which you came, that you may regain your sight and be filled with the Holy Spirit." Immediately things like scales fell from his eyes and he regained his sight.
—ACTS 9:17–18

Our conversions are often helped along by the loving hands of others. Others help us see our willfulness and the truth about ourselves. Those further along the path of listening to the voice of the Lord can guide us toward him.

Who has been instrumental in your conversion and the strengthening of your faith life? Thank them for the ways they helped remove the scales from your eyes.

Acts 22:3–16 or 9:1–22
Psalm 117
Mark 16:15–18

JANUARY 26

Anguish has taken wing, dispelled is darkness;
for there is no gloom where but now there was distress.
The people who walked in darkness
have seen a great light;
upon those who dwelt in the land of gloom
a light has shone.
—ISAIAH 8:23—9:1

A young woman was troubled. Her "land of gloom" was
mainly in her heart—a lonely marriage and the temptation to
daydream about another man. And its dark anguish crept
over her whole person like an oil spill washing out over the
once-clear ocean. But a great light came—in acceptance,
reconciliation, absolution, and grace—and rose up on the
horizon, gentle and sweet, bringing its promises of
restoration and the company of Jesus.

Isaiah 8:23—9:3
Psalm 27
1 Corinthians 1:10–13, 17
Matthew 4:12–23 or 4:12–17

"If a house is divided against itself, that house will not be able to stand."
—MARK 3:25

Jesus' tunic, for which the soldiers cast lots, was valuable because it was seamless, woven in one piece. To honor the "holy robe," pope emeritus Benedict XVI writes, "The Church Fathers saw in this the unity of the Church, founded as one indivisible community by the love of Christ . . . The Saviour's love brings together that which has been divided . . . a modest habiliment, which serves to cover the person wearing it, to protect his propriety." Christian unity is indeed meant to gather and to protect.

2 Samuel 5:1–7, 10
Psalm 89
Mark 3:22–30

JANUARY 28

• ST. THOMAS AQUINAS, PRIEST AND DOCTOR OF THE CHURCH •

Lift up, O gates, your lintels;
Reach up, you ancient portals,
that the king of glory may come in!
Who is this king of glory?
The LORD of hosts; he is the king of glory.
—PSALM 24:9–10

Thomas Aquinas, known for his intellectual acumen, was spurred on by awe. He did not allow his intellect to get in the way of his fervent love of God, but rather allowed love and awe to order his intellect. He said, "Poets and philosophers are alike in being big with wonder." Wonder in the face of the king of glory.

2 Samuel 6:12b–15, 17–19
Psalm 24
Mark 3:31–35

Wednesday

JANUARY 29

"Those sown among thorns . . . They are the people who hear the word, but worldly anxiety, the lure of riches, and the craving for other things intrude and choke the word, and it bears no fruit."
—MARK 4:18–19

Life can be thorny. And distracting. Lord, name those things which intrude upon, distort, destroy, or choke my faith. Root them out, good Jesus.

2 Samuel 7:4–17
Psalm 89
Mark 4:1–20

Thursday

JANUARY 30

"For there is nothing hidden except to be made visible; nothing is secret except to come to light."
—MARK 4:22

You've heard the phrase, "You are only as sick as your secrets." This doesn't mean you should go on a talk show and spill out your heart. However, rigorous and regular confession with the same priest over an extended period of time can bring the kind of holy illumination that heals and blesses beyond measure.

2 Samuel 7:18–19, 24–29
Psalm 132
Mark 4:21–25

Friday

JANUARY 31

• ST. JOHN BOSCO, PRIEST •

I have done such evil in your sight
that you are just in your sentence,
blameless when you condemn.
—PSALM 51:6

Maybe the story of David, Bathsheba, and Uriah seems far from us. Lust, infidelity, and murder may not be sins with which we struggle regularly, or ever. But pride, deceit, jealousy, and envy can kill the spirit just as surely as any other sin.

Lord, guard me against my own illusions. I have done evil in your sight, too. May your mercy find me.

2 Samuel 11:1–4a, 5–10a, 13–17
Psalm 51
Mark 4:26–34

FEBRUARY 1

Give me back the joy of your salvation,
and a willing spirit sustain in me.
—PSALM 51:14

Is today a day when your joy has left? When your spirit
falters and stumbles? The world can feel overwhelmingly
dark, and the trials of life can sometimes feel insurmountable.
Our great privilege as children of God is that we can turn to
the font of all joy and ask to be restored, renewed, and
sustained.

2 Samuel 12:1–7a, 10–17
Psalm 51
Mark 4:35–41

FEBRUARY 2

• THE PRESENTATION OF THE LORD •

" . . . and you yourself a sword will pierce."
—LUKE 2:35

Every human heart that has deeply, sincerely loved another understands exactly what this means. Love is piercing when it is real and rooted in heaven, when it lives not for its own sake but in complete surrender and service. There's a risk to be taken, accepted, and raised up to maturity. This is also where its power lies—to convert, to heal, and to redeem.

Lord, in this way, let me be risky and embrace the danger of loving you so well.

Malachi 3:1–4
Psalm 24
Hebrews 2:14–18
Luke 2:22–40 or 2:22–32

The LORD sustains me.
—PSALM 3:6

Is this your prayer? "Jesus, I don't think I can do it another day. I have no more strength. I have nothing left and nowhere to turn." Take a breath and remember: God is big enough for you to hit bottom. He is big enough to bring you back from wherever you may have fallen. What's more, he wants to bring you back, to restore to you all that has been lost, and he will sustain you until that work is complete.

2 Samuel 15:13–14, 30; 16:5–13
Psalm 3
Mark 5:1–20

Tuesday

FEBRUARY 4

"Do not be afraid; just have faith."
—MARK 5:36

When this seems impossible, when I'm so frustrated that I want to slam the Bible shut, when faith seems ridiculous in light of my circumstances, I try to remember the words of Jesus to the little girl: *"Talitha koum,"* "Little girl, I say to you, arise!" And I know he's speaking to me too. He is calling me out of my deep sleep of despair to rise up and walk in the light of faith again.

2 Samuel 18:9–10, 14b, 24–25a,
30—19:3
Psalm 86
Mark 5:21–43

You are my shelter; from distress you will preserve me;
with glad cries of freedom you will ring me round.
—PSALM 32:7

I was sitting there imagining that I'd made one of the biggest
mistakes of my life; some things that are done cannot be
undone. I felt great remorse and anything but free. But
somewhere deep in my bones, I clung to the belief that God
was bigger than my problem, that joy would rise up from
mourning, and that freedom would befriend me again one
day. My ability to even think this let me know I was
not alone.

2 Samuel 24:2, 9–17
Psalm 32
Mark 6:1–6

Thursday

FEBRUARY 6

• ST. PAUL MIKI AND COMPANIONS, MARTYRS •

*Jesus summoned the Twelve and began to send them out two
by two.*
—MARK 6:7

It's important and appropriate to remember that Jesus
sometimes sends us out in pairs. We need companions in the
work of evangelization; they provide company and keep us
honest and sharp. Companions remind us of our communal
call to holiness and that we are creatures designed not for
pious isolation but for divine and eternal community.

1 Kings 2:1–4, 10–12
1 Chronicles 29:10, 11b,
11d–12a, 12bcd
Mark 6:7–13

FEBRUARY 7

God's way is unerring.
—PSALM 18:31

Lord, in my staggering doubt, enfold me in the same
unwavering faith of the psalmist.

Sirach 47:2–11
Psalm 18
Mark 6:14–29

FEBRUARY 8

• ST. JEROME EMILIANI, PRIEST, ST. JOSEPHINE BAKHITA, VIRGIN •

"Give your servant . . . an understanding heart to judge your people and to distinguish right from wrong" . . .

The LORD was pleased that Solomon made this request.

—1 KINGS 3:9–10

I don't always have the heart to make noble and pure-hearted requests of God as Solomon did. I want answers and help and mercy and grace and a satisfying life. Pain and weighty responsibility come with wisdom, and maybe that's why so often we run from it.

Lord, give me the courage to ask for good and noble gifts to serve your people.

1 Kings 3:4–13
Psalm 119
Mark 6:30–34

He shall never be moved;
the just one shall be in everlasting remembrance.
An evil report he shall not fear;
his heart is firm, trusting in the LORD.
His heart is steadfast; he shall not fear.
Lavishly he gives to the poor;
his justice shall endure forever;
his horn shall be exalted in glory.
—PSALM 112:6–9

Wouldn't it be wonderful and encouraging to meet someone who is truly faithful? Someone whose heart is firm, steadfast, just? Wouldn't it be a relief to know someone like that truly exists?

Lord, make me steadfast, firm in heart, always trusting in you, that I might bring your relief to the world.

Isaiah 58:7–10
Psalm 112
1 Corinthians 2:1–5
Matthew 5:13–16

Monday

FEBRUARY 10

• ST. SCHOLASTICA, VIRGIN •

Whatever villages or towns or countryside [Jesus] entered, they laid the sick in the marketplaces and begged him that they might touch only the tassel on his cloak; and as many as touched it were healed.
—MARK 6:56

Who needs your healing touch? Who hungers for affection and embrace? Who needs you to hold their hand or help them down the steps or wipe their brow? The world has hijacked human touch for its own perverse purposes; let's not join in that attack. Reclaim your holy hands for Jesus.

1 Kings 8:1–7, 9–13
Psalm 132
Mark 6:53–56

⇒ 72 ⇐

My soul yearns and pines
for the courts of the LORD.
My heart and my flesh
cry out for the living God.
—PSALM 84:3

As I grow older, I understand this psalm more and more. My very good, very rich life unfolds, and still there is a longing that the world can never touch, no human love can supplant. There is no earthly treasure or pleasure that can distract me sufficiently from it; it is always with me, drawing me to heaven and making life all the richer and more real for it.

1 Kings 8:22–23, 27–30
Psalm 84
Mark 7:1–13

FEBRUARY 12

"What comes out of the man, that is what defiles him. From within the man, from his heart, come evil thoughts, unchastity, theft, murder, adultery, greed, malice, deceit, licentiousness, envy, blasphemy, arrogance, folly. All these evils come from within and they defile."
—MARK 7:20–23

We still place so much emphasis on what we put in our bodies and on our bodies, and some of that interest is important. But the heart is the seat of it all—wisdom or folly, generosity or greed, modesty or lust, good will or ill will. We get our hearts to the gym, but do we get them to Mass? Do we give them proper spiritual nourishment—communion and reconciliation, time in prayer and silence, a spiritual discipline aimed at growing in holiness?

1 Kings 10:1–10
Psalm 37
Mark 7:14–23

FEBRUARY 13

She came and fell at his feet.
—MARK 7:25

When all else fails, try going "nose to the floor." Jesus never once turned away from those who fell before him and sincerely begged his mercy. Not once.

1 Kings 11:4–13
Psalm 106
Mark 7:24–30

FEBRUARY 14

• ST. CYRIL, MONK; ST. METHODIUS, BISHOP •

Israel went into rebellion against David's house to this day.
—1 KINGS 12:19

The human race is no stranger to rebellion; it may be the
first and last, simplest yet deadliest of sins—that willful
turning away from the face of God. At one time or another,
in big or small ways, hardness of heart is a stumbling block
for us all. We can take solace in the fact that the "yes" of
Christ on the cross was big enough to swallow up every
human "no."

1 Kings 11:29–32; 12:19
Psalm 81
Mark 7:31–37

FEBRUARY 15

They forgot the God who had saved them,
who had done great deeds in Egypt.
—PSALM 106:21

Forgetfulness might be next on the list of great human sins.
The Israelites were masters of forgetfulness. And so am I. I
cannot count the times I have regretted my moments of
doubt and faithlessness; and I cannot think of a time when
the hand of God did not become apparent to me, working
on my behalf, perhaps long after the fact of some mysterious
difficulty or grace.

Lord, for today, I will remember you and all your marvelous,
mysterious works of mercy, pondering them in the proper
context of a whole life ordered toward eternity.

1 Kings 12:26–32; 13:33–34
Psalm 106
Mark 8:1–10

Before man are life and death, good and evil,
whichever he chooses shall be given him.
—SIRACH 15:17

It's no use trying to convince myself that I've landed where
I've landed by no cause of my own. I always have a choice,
no matter what I might tell myself. That's not to say that
choosing well is obvious or easy. Our life choices often
require input from others, along with a great deal of prayer
and fasting and patience. We make the best choices we can
with the information we are given. But there is always a way
to bring light into the darkness, if I can be patient enough
and allow God to work.

Sirach 15:15–20
Psalm 119
1 Corinthians 2:6–10
Matthew 5:17–37 or 5:20–22a, 27–28,
33–34a, 37

*But if any of you lacks wisdom, he should ask God who gives to
all generously and ungrudgingly, and he will be given it. But he
should ask in faith, not doubting, for the one who doubts is like
a wave of the sea that is driven and tossed about by the wind.
For that person must not suppose that he will receive anything
from the Lord, since he is a man of two minds, unstable in all
his ways.*
—JAMES 1:5–8

Lord, make me of one mind, give me singleness of purpose,
and an undivided heart.

James 1:1–11
Psalm 119
Mark 8:11–13

FEBRUARY 18

When sin reaches maturity it gives birth to death.
—JAMES 1:15

Which is another way to say, do not let sin mother you.
Reject its attempts to nurture life habits that actually
bring death.

James 1:12–18
Psalm 94
Mark 8:14–21

Everyone should be quick to hear, slow to speak and slow to anger for anger does not accomplish the righteousness of God.
—JAMES 1:19–20

The unbridled tongue, energized by the undisciplined heart, has probably done more damage to more people than any other weapon on earth.

Lord, teach me when to speak and when to be silent, when to act and when to listen.

James 1:19–27
Psalm 15
Mark 8:22–26

FEBRUARY 20

If you fulfill the royal law according to the Scripture, "You shall love your neighbor as yourself," you are doing well.
—JAMES 2:8

A reporter once recounted this story about Dorothy Day. He'd come to interview her and entered the room where she sat talking with an elderly man who'd clearly been living on the street. She looked up at the reporter and asked, "Did you want to speak to one of us?" He was struck by her lack of presumption. Of course, both she and this homeless man were of equal importance; indeed, every neighbor has his story to tell.

James 2:1–9
Psalm 34
Mark 8:27–33

Light shines through the darkness for the upright.
—PSALM 112:4

I knew a man cloaked in darkness, waiting for God to strike him hopeful, imagining that God would force himself on him without invitation. That's poor theology. Darkness will fall on the righteous and unrighteous alike. The difference is that the upright, by their interior posture, invite light, invite grace, and cooperate with the hand of God. The upright accept their part to become honest, open, and willing to allow God to change them.

Live as an invitation to light, to grace, to holy change.

James 2:14–24, 26
Psalm 112
Mark 8:34—9:1

Saturday

FEBRUARY 22

• THE CHAIR OF ST. PETER, APOSTLE •

Tend the flock of God in your midst, overseeing not by constraint but willingly . . . not for shameful profit but eagerly. Do not lord it over those assigned to you, but be examples to the flock.
—1 PETER 5:2–3

Christian leadership is not driven by power or profit, but by tenderness, fidelity, and service.

Today, we keep our Church leaders in prayer, remembering by name our parish priests.

1 Peter 5:1–4
Psalm 23
Matthew 16:13–19

FEBRUARY 23

"You shall not bear hatred for your brother or sister in your heart. Though you may have to reprove your fellow citizen, do not incur sin because of him. Take no revenge and cherish no grudge against any of your people. You shall love your neighbor as yourself. I am the LORD."
—LEVITICUS 19:17–18

Grudges and resentment are serious offenses. They might be understandable, but we cannot dabble with them or give them any sway whatsoever. At the same time, we are not expected to be doormats but to challenge our sisters and brothers when they sin against us. It is a spiritual work of mercy to admonish sinners, a work that should be cloaked not in a desire to be right, but in prayer and wise counsel and hearts truly interested in the most honest and loving outcome.

Leviticus 19:1–2, 17–18
Psalm 103
1 Corinthians 3:16–23
Matthew 5:38–48

FEBRUARY 24

"This kind can only come out through prayer."
—MARK 9:29

The story of Jesus healing the young boy possessed by a demon is less a demonstration of the apostles' failure and more a reminder of prayer's power. A man I know in the hospital with a life-threatening illness says he can do nothing at all—has not even the energy to sit up. "All I can do," he says, "is pray." He may be the most powerful man on earth.

James 3:13–18
Psalm 19
Mark 9:14–29

*Resist the Devil, and he will flee from you. Draw near to God,
and he will draw near to you.*
—JAMES 4:7–8

How much resistance does it take to make the devil flee? Too
often I give the devil far too much credit and attribute to him
far more power than he possesses. If I can only resist with the
strength of a wilted tulip, it's enough. God will rush in and
do all the rest. He will draw near. When all I can offer is the
desire to resist, it's enough. God will draw near.

James 4:1–10
Psalm 55
Mark 9:30–37

Wednesday

FEBRUARY 26

*You have no idea what your life will be like tomorrow. You are a
puff of smoke that appears briefly and then disappears. Instead
you should say, "If the Lord wills it . . ."*
—JAMES 4:14–15

Sometimes it's just the right medicine to be smacked down to
size. From one puff of smoke to another, it is a great relief to
know I live in this day only. And Lord willing, I will make it a
holy and good one.

James 4:13–17
Psalm 49
Mark 9:38–40

Behold, the wages you withheld from the workers who harvested your fields are crying aloud; and the cries of the harvesters have reached the ears of the Lord of hosts.
—JAMES 5:4

What is the wage that I owe, and to whom do I owe it? Have I withheld affection, tenderness, financial support, material resources, my time, my prayers, or my listening ear from someone who deserves it, has earned it? Who suffers the neglect of my unmet obligations and cries out to the Lord?

James 5:1–6
Psalm 49
Mark 9:41–50

FEBRUARY 28

They are no longer two but one flesh.
—MARK 10:8

When I read this passage as a newlywed, it took on new meaning. Not about sex—or not only about sex—but about the reality of building a life with someone. Something new is born between us—the love we have for each other is a new creation, and we are now bound to one another in a sacramental reality that is borne out in daily reality, our complementarity, our habits and choices, and the proper friction that is created when living creatures encounter one another.

James 5:9–12
Psalm 103
Mark 10:1–12

*The fervent prayer of a righteous person is very powerful. Elijah
was a man like us; yet he prayed earnestly that it might not rain,
and for three years and six months it did not rain . . . Then
Elijah prayed again, and the sky gave rain and the earth
produced its fruit.*
—JAMES 5:16–18

Is God swayed? Changeable? Under the influence of
fervency? Perhaps we should focus not on the power of
Elijah's prayer as much as on the power of the One who
answered it. When we consider that God Almighty chooses
to collaborate with his creation, all our prayers might
become more fervent and give us power, with God's grace, to
move heaven and earth toward every good thing.

James 5:13–20
Psalm 141
Mark 10:13–16

He will bring to light what is hidden in darkness and will manifest the motives of our hearts.
—1 CORINTHIANS 4:5

This is a promise, a reassurance, and a reminder. Ultimately, no one gets to hide, and this is a great mercy. Privacy is from Jesus; secrecy is from the devil. Privacy protects the person; secrecy corrodes human dignity.

Isaiah 49:14–15
Psalm 62
1 Corinthians 4:1–5
Matthew 6:24–34

Blessed be God and Father of our Lord Jesus Christ, who in his great mercy gave us a new birth to a living hope through the resurrection of Jesus Christ from the dead, to an inheritance that is imperishable, undefiled, and unfading, kept in heaven for you who by the power of God are safeguarded through faith.
—1 PETER 1:3–5

Directions: read slowly aloud. "Great mercy, living hope, resurrection from the dead, an imperishable, undefiled, unfading inheritance kept in heaven for you, who is safeguarded by the power of God."

Repeat as needed.

1 Peter 1:3–9
Psalm 111
Mark 10:17–27

Tuesday

MARCH 4

• ST. CASIMIR •

Gird up the loins of your mind, live soberly, and set your hopes completely on the grace to be brought to you at the revelation of Jesus Christ.
—1 PETER 1:13

Blessed John Henry Newman said it this way: "I want a laity . . . who know their religion, who enter into it, who know just where they stand, who know what they hold, and what they do not, who know their creed so well, that they can give an account of it, who know so much of history that they can defend it. I want an intelligent, well-instructed laity . . . I wish you to enlarge your knowledge, to cultivate your reason, to get an insight into the relation of truth to truth, to learn to view things as they are, to understand how faith and reason stand to each other."

1 Peter 1:10–16
Psalm 98
Mark 10:28–31

Wednesday

MARCH 5

• ASH WEDNESDAY •

Proclaim a fast.
—JOEL 2:15

Our readings exhort us to fast, also, to take care to hide our
fasting. Yet today we will walk around in public marked by
ashes. It is good to remember that the proclamation Joel
speaks of is a unifying one; we do our fasting not just as
individuals, but as the Church body. We come together in
our acts of repentance to help one another return to the Lord
wholeheartedly.

Joel 2:12–18
Psalm 51
2 Corinthians 5:20—6:2
Matthew 6:1–6, 16–18

Thursday

MARCH 6

"Choose life, then, that you and your descendants may live, by loving the LORD, your God, heeding his voice, and holding fast to him. For that will mean life for you, a long life for you."
—DEUTERONOMY 30:19–20

What does it mean to choose life? How will I, with intention and resolve, with courage and boldness, choose life today?

Deuteronomy 30:15–20
Psalm 1
Luke 9:22–25

This, rather, is the fasting that I wish:
releasing those bound unjustly,
untying the thongs of the yoke;
Setting free the oppressed,
breaking every yoke;
Sharing your bread with the hungry,
sheltering the oppressed and the homeless;
Clothing the naked when you see them,
and not turning your back on your own.
Then your light shall break forth like the dawn,
and your wound shall quickly be healed.
—ISAIAH 58:6–8

Do I fast only in terms of giving up something I enjoy? This
Lent, is my fasting active, bound up in forgiveness, justice,
generosity, care for others, and fidelity?

Isaiah 58:1–9a
Psalm 51
Matthew 9:14–15

If you remove from your midst oppression,
false accusation and malicious speech;
If you bestow your bread on the hungry and satisfy the afflicted;
Then light shall rise for you in the darkness, . . .
He will renew your strength,
and you shall be like a watered garden,
like a spring whose water never fails.
—ISAIAH 58:9–11

Truth is attractive in itself; virtue needs no marketing campaign. We would do well to sit with Isaiah's images: lush and inviting gardens, light rising in the darkness. Hope and refreshment always seem to accompany goodness.

Isaiah 58:9b–14
Psalm 86
Luke 5:27–32

⇒ 98 ⇐

Sunday

MARCH 9

• FIRST SUNDAY OF LENT •

The LORD God formed man out of the clay of the ground and
blew into his nostrils the breath of life, and so man became a
living being.
—GENESIS 2:7

Life is a gift—mysterious and beautiful and a cause for great
wonder. This year, let us offer some of our Lenten fasting for
those who attack life through war, abortion, euthanasia, or
forced sterilizations and for those whose lives are especially
vulnerable—the unborn, the elderly, and the sick.

Lord, my life is a gift from you. May I return it to you with
gratitude to do with as you will.

Genesis 2:7–9; 3:1–7
Psalm 51
Romans 5:12–19 or 5:12, 17–19
Matthew 4:1–11

Monday
MARCH 10

Let the words of my mouth and the thought of my heart
find favor before you,
O LORD.
—PSALM 19:15

Much of what flows from the lips begins first in the heart.
Lord, give me a thinking heart, one constantly renewed and
refreshed by your words, your sacraments, holy friendships,
and a life spent constantly returning to you.

Leviticus 19:1–2, 11–18
Psalm 19
Matthew 25:31–46

MARCH 11

"hallowed be thy name."
—MATTHEW 6:9

Wonderful counselor, Prince of Peace, Teacher, Rabboni!
Savior, Lord, Crucified One, Messiah.
My healer, my friend, my comforter.
Light of the world, "I AM."
Mercy.
Father, Son, Spirit, Trinity, God Almighty.
Creator of all things visible and invisible, Holy One, Lord of
All, Emmanuel, Breath of heaven.
Jesus.
How do you know him? How would you like to know him
better? Pick one name and spend extra time meditating on it
during this Lenten season.

Isaiah 55:10–11
Psalm 34
Matthew 6:7–15

*My sacrifice, O God, is a contrite spirit;
a heart contrite and humbled, O God, you will not spurn.*
—PSALM 51:19

Contrition is hard. Who wants to grieve the full weight of
their own sin? Lent gives us the opportunity to focus more
on contrition and penitence not because the Church is bent
on our unhappiness, but because she is deeply invested in our
freedom. Contrition leads to freedom—a freedom to love
that cannot be touched by governments or the control and
judgments of others. Lent helps lift us out of sin's slavery to
live with the freedom that protects and expands our capacity
to love well.

Jonah 3:1–10
Psalm 51
Luke 11:29–32

"Put in my mouth persuasive words in the presence of the lion."
—ESTHER C:24

Ella's boss was brilliant and very abusive. Ella would spend
time with Queen Esther before she went into meetings with
him, asking God to give her "eloquent speech before the
lion." We all have our lions. Esther is a wonderful model for
those moments when we find ourselves frightened by a
difficult conversation we know we must have.

Jehovah, put eloquent speech in my mouth before the lion.

Esther C:12, 14–16, 23–25
Psalm 138
Matthew 7:7–12

If you bring your gift to the altar, and there recall that your brother has anything against you, leave your gift there at the altar, go first and be reconciled with your brother, and then come and offer your gift.
—MATTHEW 5:23–24

This is an ongoing process—forgiving and being forgiven, working out resentments, reconciling with one another. The goal is to develop a heart habituated to seeking reconciliation. It is important to mean what we say and to live with integrity as best we can, understanding that there is an order to the life of that spirit that must be properly reverenced.

Ezekiel 18:21–28
Psalm 130
Matthew 5:20–26

MARCH 15

"Love your enemies, and pray for those who persecute you."
—MATTHEW 5:44

If only I would love my enemies. We remember Jesus' words
on the cross. He doesn't say, "Lord, I forgive them and all is
well." He says, "Forgive them, Lord, they know not what
they do." It's almost a request. We can turn to the Lord and
ask him to do the forgiving first, and through him, we can
follow suit. It is through the forgiving heart of God that we
can love our enemies in both prayer and action.

Deuteronomy 26:16–19
Psalm 119
Matthew 5:43–48

Sunday

MARCH 16

• SECOND SUNDAY OF LENT •

All the communities of the earth shall find blessing in you.
—GENESIS 12:3

To bless: to consecrate, to make holy, to invoke divine care for, to speak well of, to confer prosperity or happiness upon, to protect, preserve, endow, favor.

This is your heritage: you are blessed—made holy, held in divine hands, protected, favored—that others may find blessing in you.

Do I live a blessed life? Do others find blessing in me?

Genesis 12:1–4a
Psalm 33
2 Timothy 1:8b–10
Matthew 17:1–9

"Give and gifts will be given to you; a good measure, packed together, shaken down, and overflowing, will be poured into your lap."
—LUKE 6:38

Lord, what are you asking me to give in this season? My time, my resources, my energy? Or perhaps forgiveness long overdue, greater charity to my family or someone who has hurt me, my support in prayer and attention to those in need around me? What may I give for love of you?

Daniel 9:4b–10
Psalm 79
Luke 6:36–38

Tuesday

MARCH 18

• ST. CYRIL OF JERUSALEM, BISHOP AND DOCTOR OF THE CHURCH •

Put away your misdeeds from before my eyes;
cease doing evil; learn to do good.
Make justice your aim; redress the wronged,
hear the orphan's plea, defend the widow.
—ISAIAH 1:16–17

The prophet tells us, essentially, "Do some service for
someone else." It is a powerful antidote to selfishness, fear,
pride, and any assortment of difficulties of the human heart.
Place your focus and energy at the behest of someone who
needs you. Are you caught up in some difficulty, some sin?
Having difficulty putting away some evil in your life?
Service, even the most hidden or minor, might be just
the thing.

Isaiah 1:10, 16–20
Psalm 50
Matthew 23:1–12

Wednesday

MARCH 19

• ST. JOSEPH, HUSBAND OF THE BLESSED VIRGIN MARY •

He is our father . . . who gives life to the dead and calls into
being what does not exist.
—ROMANS 4:17

As Emmet Fox notes, "[Our Father] tells all that man needs to
know about God, and about himself, and about his
neighbor. . . . In this [name] Jesus lays down once and for all
that the relationship between God and man is that of Father
and child. This eliminates any possibility that the Deity
could be the relentless and cruel tyrant."

Spend some time today thanking God for the fathers, father
figures, and protectors in your life.

2 Samuel 7:4–5a, 12–14a, 16
Psalm 89
Romans 4:13, 16–18, 22
Matthew 1:16, 18–21, 24a or
Luke 2:41–51a

More torturous than all else is the human heart,
beyond remedy; who can understand it?
I, the LORD, alone probe the mind
and test the heart.
—JEREMIAH 17:9–10

It is one kind of pain to be misunderstood by another; it's something else when I, at times, don't even understand myself. In this torturous condition, Lord, help me know myself. I trust that you know me and are leading me out of darkness and confusion into light and clarity.

Jeremiah 17:5–10
Psalm 1
Luke 16:19–31

MARCH 21

*When the chief priests and the Pharisees heard his parables,
they knew that he was speaking about them.*
—MATTHEW 21:45

It is rarely the case that I can plead ignorance; just like the
Pharisees, I know my own sin. I choose it, and I plot against
the Truth in some way or another. I scuttle about, trying to
avoid myself and trying to justify myself when I have
behaved hypocritically, falsely, or meanly. When I am
tempted to put more distance between me and the Pharisee
than is honest, I can ask for God's grace to live in reality. I
can trust that if I turn to him, I can be healed of hypocrisy.

Genesis 37:3–4, 12–13a, 17b–28a
Psalm 105
Matthew 21:33–43, 45–46

Saturday

MARCH 22

You will cast into the depths of the sea all our sins.
—MICAH 7:19

Henri Nouwen writes, "God's forgiveness is unconditional; it comes from a heart that does not demand anything for itself, a heart that is completely empty of self-seeking. It is this divine forgiveness that I have to practice in my daily life. It calls me to keep stepping over all my arguments that say forgiveness is unwise, unhealthy, and impractical. It challenges me to step over all my needs for gratitude and compliments. Finally it demands of me that I step over that wounded part of my heart that feels hurt and wronged and wants to stay in control and put a few conditions between me and the one whom I am asked to forgive."

Micah 7:14–15, 18–20
Psalm 103
Luke 15:1–3, 11–32

"Come see a man who told me everything I have done."
—JOHN 4:29

She was a woman of faith and of flaws. You wonder if she
was embarrassed, ashamed, amazed, or afraid. Revelation
always marks these early encounters with Christ. He reveals
himself as he reveals the woman with five husbands to
herself. But revelation—revealing, uncovering, exposing
us—is always meant to bring us into reality. He reveals these
things, not to condemn us, but to free us through our
repentance and his healing grace.

Exodus 17:3–7
Psalm 95
Romans 5:1–2, 5–8
John 4:5–42 or 4:5–15, 19b–26, 39a,
40–42

Monday

MARCH 24

As the hind longs for the running waters,
so my soul longs for you, O God.
Athirst is my soul for God, the living God.
When shall I go and behold the face of God?
—PSALM 42:2–3

"As adults," writes Don Briel, "we distance ourselves from our longings. We operate out of a fundamental detachment, fearing that we might lose ourselves in our desire for the other. We emphasize the adult virtues of temperance and prudence, and it may well be that these virtues . . . are obstacles to the kingdom. They isolate us from that which we desire, and so . . . we define ourselves in isolation from, rather than in relation to, that which we seek, that which we love."

2 Kings 5:1–15ab
Psalm 42, 43
Luke 4:24–30

MARCH 25

• THE ANNUNCIATION OF THE LORD •

Mary said, "Behold, I am the handmaid of the Lord. May it be done to me according to your word."
—LUKE 1:38

Caryll Houselander writes, "When our Lady stood up, a queenly child, and uttered her fiat to the Angel of God, her words began to make Christ's voice. Those first words of consent had already spoken Christ's last words of consent; her 'I commit myself to you, do whatever you like with me' were already spoken by Christ in her; they were one and the same with His 'Father, into thy hands I commend my spirit' . . . God asks extreme courage in love."

Isaiah 7:10–14; 8:10
Psalm 40
Hebrews 10:4–10
Luke 1:26–38

Wednesday

MARCH 26

"Take care and be earnestly on your guard not to forget the things which your own eyes have seen, nor let them slip from your memory as long as you live, but teach them to your children and to your children's children."
—DEUTERONOMY 4:9

Teach what you know of God also to your neighbor and your co-worker, through your example and the way you lead a shining life for Jesus. Teach it to your legislators and your government in the way you help speak for the poor, the vulnerable, the elderly, the unborn, and others who cannot speak for themselves. Teach, with gentle clarity and strength, to those who are placed on the path of your life. Teach what you remember of God's shining works and Christ's truth.

Deuteronomy 4:1, 5–9
Psalm 147
Matthew 5:17–19

Thursday

MARCH 27

They walked in the hardness of their evil hearts and turned their backs, not their faces, to me.
—JEREMIAH 7:24

My hardness of heart generally resides in one of two places: unwillingness to forgive someone who has hurt me or unwillingness to admit I am wrong. They are often related; willfulness has a big family, many siblings, cousins, sons, and daughters. But as I grow older (perhaps because I've had more opportunity), it becomes easier to admit when I'm wrong and to pray for that inward turning toward the pure, piercing, and perfect heart of God.

Jeremiah 7:23–28
Psalm 95
Luke 11:14–23

I will heal their defection, says the LORD,
I will love them freely.
—HOSEA 14:5

Freedom to love well and to love rightly is the only real
freedom there is. All the healing I need is related to this.
Every defect of my character stands as an obstacle to loving
well, loving rightly, loving deeply and unselfishly. God's love
for me, however, is perfectly free. It knows no obstacle, is
completely unfettered, and is willing to go to any length to
find me and draw me home.

Hosea 14:2–10
Psalm 81
Mark 12:28–34

*For it is love that I desire, not sacrifice,
and knowledge of God rather than burnt offerings.*
—HOSEA 6:6

In the Gospel reading, the Pharisee brings his account to
God: "I fast, I pray, I tithe, I am not like the rest of greedy,
dishonest, adulterous humanity." But the tax collector brings
his heart: he lowers his eyes and beats his breast and begs for
mercy. "O God, be merciful to me a sinner." It is as simple
as that.

Hosea 6:1–6
Psalm 51
Luke 18:9–14

MARCH 30

Sunday

• FOURTH SUNDAY OF LENT •

"Not as man sees does God see, because man sees the
appearance but the LORD looks into the heart."
—1 SAMUEL 16:7

Lord, look into my heart. I am frightened and weak, weary
and faint with despair. Look into my heart, O Lord. How I
need you! I have been abandoned, rejected, forgotten. Lord,
see my heart, see how I struggle with sin, with worry, with
loneliness, with pride. Lord, see me. See me and save me.

1 Samuel 16:1b, 6–7, 10–13a
Psalm 23
Ephesians 5:8–14
John 9:1–41 or 9:1, 6–9, 13–17, 34–48

Jesus said to him, "You may go; your son will live." The man believed what Jesus said to him and left. . . . Now this was the second sign Jesus did when he came to Galilee from Judea.
—JOHN 4:50, 54

The first miracle was changing water into wine at the wedding feast of Cana. The second was healing a child from a deathly fever—and more than that, it was answering the prayer of a father for his son. Here is the power of a praying parent—first Mary intervening at the wedding feast, then a father interceding for his child. What is Jesus teaching us about family and prayer in these signs and wonders?

Isaiah 65:17–21
Psalm 30
John 4:43–54

God is our refuge and our strength,
an ever-present help in distress.
Therefore we fear not, though the earth be shaken
and mountains plunge into the depths of the sea.
—PSALM 46:1

What's your plunging mountain, your shaking earth?
Financial ruin? Divorce? Betrayal? Has someone told lies
about your character or revealed your private affairs? Did
someone lie to you, someone you truly trusted, someone you
believed? The world will shake and sometimes crumble down
upon us, but God alone will never fail nor leave us. God will
be your refuge.

Ezekiel 47:1–9, 12
Psalm 46
John 5:1–16

Wednesday

APRIL 2

• ST. FRANCIS OF PAOLA, HERMIT •

*"I cannot do anything on my own; I judge as I hear, and my
judgment is just, because I do not seek my own will but the will
of the one who sent me."*
—JOHN 5:30

It can be tempting to think of Jesus as an individualist, a
tough resistor who carves out his own path. But we must
never forget that the source of his strength and the justice of
his judgment issue from the Father. Jesus' will and the will of
the Father are one; the Trinity is a community. Willfulness
disguised as individualism, martyrdom, or even holiness is
simply a spiritual temper tantrum, and it severs all that draws
us to the Father.

Isaiah 49:8–15
Psalm 145
John 5:17–30

Thursday

APRIL 3

"You search the Scriptures, because you think you have eternal life through them; even they testify on my behalf. But you do not want to come to me to have life."
—JOHN 5:39–40

Catherine of Siena once wrote that the Lord "hates above all things three abominable sins, covetousness, unchastity and pride."

If I am experiencing resistance toward Jesus, are any of these sins behind that resistance?

Exodus 32:7–14
Psalm 106
John 5:31–47

APRIL 4

• ST. ISIDORE, BISHOP AND DOCTOR OF THE CHURCH •

Their wickedness blinded them.
—WISDOM 2:21

Blindness often comes bit by bit. Immorality is not something in which we can occasionally dabble without too much trouble. Evil is not stagnant; rather, it eats away at the very gifts we are given to navigate the world well. The creep of evil prevents our enjoyment of life, work, friendship, family, and love.

Wisdom 2:1a, 12–22
Psalm 34
John 7:1–2, 10, 25–30

Yet I, like a trusting lamb led to slaughter,
had not realized that they were hatching plots against me.
—JEREMIAH 11:19

If someone takes advantage of you or plots to harm you, or if you trusted and were betrayed, do not conclude that it's wrong to trust. Trust is a highly favored daughter in the family of virtue, and she is not only given, but earned.

If need be, ask Jesus to restore your trust in him first, and then you can work together on trusting others.

Jeremiah 11:18–20
Psalm 7
John 7:40–53

She said to him, "Yes, Lord. I have come to believe that you are the Christ, the Son of God, the one who is coming into the world."
—JOHN 11:27

Many of our conversion stories are sprinkled with dramatic, watershed moments, but for the most part, changes of heart unfold over time, as we persist in prayer and the sacraments and as we pursue the truth in study, friendship, and vocation.

We come to believe just as Mary did, in the process of building a relationship with Christ. He comes into our world in daily encounters with truth and love.

Ezekiel 37:12–14
Psalm 130
Romans 8:8–11
John 11:1–45 or 11:3–7, 17, 20–27,
33b–45

APRIL 7

• ST. JOHN BAPTIST DE LA SALLE, PRIEST •

*"Let the one among you who is without sin be the first to throw
a stone at her."*
—JOHN 8:7

In the Old Testament reading, we have Susanna, the
innocent, accused. In the Gospel, we have the adulteress
woman "caught in the act," forgiven. The contrast is
interesting; both women are protected from death. And this
is truly at the heart of heaven; no matter where we fall on the
line of holiness, we are protected, forgiven, and drawn nearer
to life with God.

Daniel 13:1–9, 15–17, 19–30, 33–62
or 13:41c–62
Psalm 23
John 8:1–11

Tuesday

APRIL 8

*O LORD hear my prayer,
and let my cry come to you.
Hide not your face from me
in the day of my distress.
Incline your ear to me;
in the day when I call, answer me speedily.*
—PSALM 102:2–3

No matter how often I pray this, I notice that speed is not exactly of interest to heaven. Conversion is though, and that is a long and exacting work.

Lord, I know you are here with me. I know you hear my cry, and I trust in your provision, guidance, and grace, whatever forms they may take.

Numbers 21:4–9
Psalm 102
John 8:21–30

If our God, who we serve, can save us from the white-hot furnace and from your hands, O king, may he save us! But even if he will not, know, O king, that we will not serve your god or worship the golden statue that you set up.
—DANIEL 3:17–18

Shadrach, Meshach, and Abednego possess a kind of courage we need very much in these days. My love and faithfulness are too often tied to a "successful" outcome—greater safety, reassurance, or affirmation. And yet, "even if he will not save me," even if greater safety, reassurance, affirmation or consolation does not come, will my loyalty waver? How would my life change if I were willing to walk into the white-hot furnace?

Daniel 3:14–20, 91–92, 95
Daniel 3:52, 53, 54, 55, 56
John 8:31–42

Thursday

APRIL 10

When Abram prostrated himself, God spoke to him.
—GENESIS 17:3

Was Abram's posture important? Does it matter that we sit,
kneel, or stand when we approach God? Does it matter what
we wear to Mass on Sundays? Is an outward sign ever the
catalyst for God's action? Is God moved by our little or great
acts of devotion?

Genesis 17:3–9
Psalm 105
John 8:51–59

Friday

APRIL 11

• ST. STANISLAUS, BISHOP AND MARTYR •

I love you, O LORD, my strength.
—PSALM 18:2

I love you, Lord, my help, my life, my guiding grace, my friend, my deliverer, my shield, my Lord.

Sometimes, it's just enough to say, "I love you."

Jeremiah 20:10–13
Psalm 18
John 10:31–42

Saturday

APRIL 12

I will turn their mourning into joy.
—JEREMIAH 31:13

Joy is simply sorrow all grown up in God's grace.

Ezekiel 37:21–28
Jeremiah 31:10, 11–12abcd, 13
John 11:45–56

"Take and eat; this is my body."
—MATTHEW 26:26

The words *consume* and *consummate* have the same Latin
root. Inherent in their meaning is the idea of completion,
perfection, and fulfillment. Indeed, the Eucharist is the
fulfillment of God's perfect self-giving through Christ. In
perfect and complete self-giving, we allow ourselves to be
consumed, to be brought to completion and fulfillment.

Matthew 21:1–11
Isaiah 50:4–7
Psalm 22
Philippians 2:6–11
Matthew 26:14—27:66 or 27:11–54

Monday

APRIL 14

Thus says God, the LORD,
who created the heavens and stretched them out,
. . . I have grasped you by the hand;
I formed you, and set you
as a covenant of the people,
a light for the nations,
To open the eyes of the blind,
to bring out prisoners from confinement,
and from the dungeon, those who live in darkness.
—ISAIAH 42:5–7

Do I walk through the world as though the Almighty has grasped my hand, as if I have been given my life's work by the one who created the heavens and stretched them, vast and glorious, across the universe?

Isaiah 42:1–7
Psalm 27
John 12:1–11

Tuesday

APRIL 15

The LORD called me from birth,
from my mother's womb he gave me my name.
—ISAIAH 49:1

Isaiah wouldn't have understood the notion of "identity crisis." If we allow God to name us and claim us, neither will we suffer from a crisis of identity.

I will remind myself periodically throughout the day that I have been named and claimed by God Almighty as his son or daughter.

Isaiah 49:1–6
Psalm 71
John 13:21–33, 36–38

———————————

⇒ 136 ⇐

Wednesday

APRIL 16

Insult has broken my heart.
—PSALM 69:21

When your heart is broken—and if you're a living human being, it will break—trust that Jesus can use even your broken heart to bring new life to you and to those around you. It is his business to rebuild all those who are broken—in heart, mind, body, spirit. Let the Lord rebuild all that has been broken in you.

Lord, I invite your restoration and healing.

Isaiah 50:4–9a
Psalm 69
Matthew 26:14–25

Thursday

APRIL 17

• HOLY THURSDAY •

Jesus knew that his hour had come.
—JOHN 13:1

When his hour had come, Jesus bent low and washed his disciples' feet, saying, "I have given you a model to follow, so that as I have done for you, you should also do."

Has your hour come? Is Jesus asking you to bend low, humble yourself, and serve in some way that seems impossible, nonsensical, or humiliating?

CHRISM MASS:
Isaiah 61:1–3ab, 6a, 8b–9
Psalm 89
Revelation 1:5–8
Luke 4:16–21

EVENING MASS OF THE
LORD'S SUPPER:
Exodus 12:1–8, 11–14
Psalm 116
1 Corinthians 11:23–26
John 13:1–15

Friday

APRIL 18

• GOOD FRIDAY OF THE LORD'S PASSION •

But he was pierced for our offenses,
crushed for our sins;
upon him was the chastisement that makes us whole,
by his stripes we were healed.
—ISAIAH 53:5

Blessed John Henry Newman tells us, "Think of the Cross when you rise and when you lie down, when you go out and when you come in, when you eat and when you walk and when you converse, when you buy and when you sell, when you labour and when you rest, consecrating and sealing all your doings with this one mental action, the thought of the Crucified." Yes, and the healing he brings.

Isaiah 52:13—53:12
Psalm 31
Hebrews 4:14–16; 5:7–9
John 18:1—19:42

Saturday

APRIL 19

• HOLY SATURDAY •

"Like a wife forsaken and grieved in spirit,
a wife married . . . and then cast off, . . . /
But with great tenderness I will take you back."
—ISAIAH 54:6–7

Abandonment says, "You do not exist to me; you and your needs are of no consequence." It is a pain unlike any other. But the Easter Vigil, like the gentle rising of dawn, is the surest proof of our value before heaven, and the lengths the Father will go to say, "You are my beloved."

EASTER VIGIL:
Genesis 1:1—2:2 or 1:1, 26–31a
Psalm 104 or Psalm 33
Genesis 22:1–18 or 22:1–2, 9a, 10–13, 15–18
Psalm 16
Exodus 14:15—15:1
Exodus 15:1–2, 3–4, 5–6, 17–18
Isaiah 54:5–14
Psalm 30

Isaiah 55:1–11
Isaiah 12:2–3, 4, 5–6
Baruch 3:9–15, 32—4:4
Psalm 19
Ezekiel 36:16–17a, 18–28
Psalm 42—43 or Isaiah 12 or Psalm 51
Romans 6:3–11
Psalm 118
Matthew 28:1–10

Sunday

APRIL 20

• EASTER SUNDAY—THE RESURRECTION OF THE LORD •

He saw and believed.
—JOHN 20:8

A faithful couple I know struggled with infertility. They tried everything and chased every possible treatment. Just when they'd about given up all hope, the wife woke up feeling nauseous. Months passed and ultrasounds followed; there were fingers and toes and a nose and occasional kicks in the belly. And life. When all logic had been exhausted and only the faintest, nonsensical hope remained, there came that relentless little heartbeat.

Jesus, we come to the empty tomb; help us believe.

Acts 10:34a, 37–43
Psalm 118
Colossians 3:1–4 or
1 Corinthians 5:6b–8
John 20:1–9 or Matthew 28:1–10
Or, at afternoon or evening Mass,
Luke 24:13–35

Monday

APRIL 21

*Mary Magdalene and the other Mary went away quickly from
the tomb, fearful yet overjoyed.*
—MATTHEW 28:8

We mustn't forget how bewildering the resurrection must
have been to those early disciples. When we find ourselves
bewildered, facing a maelstrom of emotions—joy and fear
and puzzlement—we needn't be overly worried. It's very
human to meet mystery of this magnitude with a mixture of
emotions and wonder. But it's only a place to start. Jesus can
take that and grow it into the fullness of faith.

Acts 2:14, 22–33
Psalm 16
Matthew 28:8–15

Now when they heard this, they were cut to the heart, and they asked Peter and the other Apostles, "What are we to do, my brothers?" Peter said to them, "Repent and be baptized . . . in the name of Jesus Christ, for the forgiveness of your sins; and you will receive the gift of the Holy Spirit."
—ACTS 2:37–38

Truth cuts to the heart because that's where it lives. Always our response must be to bend in truth's direction, to surrender to it, whatever it might be. What was Peter's way of saying this? "Repent and be baptized for the forgiveness of your sins." This is always going to be the way forward.

Acts 2:36–41
Psalm 33
John 20:11–18

*Peter and John were going up to the temple area for the three
o'clock hour of prayer.*
—ACTS 3:1

It is in the midst of a normal day—a holy life ordered toward
the rhythms of prayer and sacraments—when grace and
healing are unleashed. Just like the man crippled from birth,
we are raised up and healed in the grace of daily-ness
ordered toward heaven.

Acts 3:1–10
Psalm 105
Luke 24:13–35

The disciples of Jesus recounted what had taken place along the way, and how they had come to recognize him in the breaking of the bread.
—LUKE 24:35

Do *I* recognize him in the breaking of the bread, the celebration of the Holy Mass, the prayers of consecration: this is my Body, given up for you?

Acts 3:11–26
Psalm 8
Luke 24:35–48

⇒ 145 ⇐

*There is no salvation through anyone else, nor is there any
other name under heaven given to the human race by which we
are to be saved.*
—ACTS 4:12

Jesus, I speak your name. I wrap my family, my loved ones,
my work, my will, my fears and worries, my hopes and heart
in the mantle of your holy name.

Acts 4:1–12
Psalm 118
John 21:1–14

*As the Eleven were at table, he appeared to them and rebuked
them for their unbelief and hardness of heart.*
—MARK 16:14

Unbelief and hardness of heart are the sins of the Eleven, the
highly elect, those chosen to go out to the whole world and
"proclaim the Gospel to every creature." We needn't be so
shocked when those to whom we have been entrusted—our
shepherds—suffer hardness of heart and failure of every
kind. We must meet the humanity and fallen nature of our
brethren and ourselves with tenacity, with steadfast and
gentle rebuke, and courage.

Acts 4:13–21
Psalm 118
Mark 16:9–15

Jesus came and stood in their midst and said to them, "Peace be with you."
—JOHN 20:19

His first gift to the frightened, bewildered disciples is *peace*, the peace of his very presence. He is still in our midst, bringing his peace—in the Eucharist, in the sacraments and every prayer, in our loneliness and joy, in mercy and grace and forgiveness. And in one another.

Lord, be in my midst. Help me receive your peace and offer it to all around me.

Acts 2:42–47
Psalm 118
1 Peter 1:3–9
John 20:19–31

*As they prayed, the place where they were gathered shook, and
they were all filled with the Holy Spirit.*
—ACTS 4:31

Maybe the earth doesn't quake when you pray; that doesn't
mean the Holy Spirit is not present, longing to fill you right
now with the same boldness and clarity of heart that was
bestowed on those early apostles.

Acts 4:23–31
Psalm 2
John 3:1–8

*"Amen, amen, I say to you, we speak of what we know and we
testify to what we have seen."*
—JOHN 3:11

In St. Catherine's *Dialogues*, Jesus spoke to her, saying,
"Daughter, do you know who you are and who I am? If you
know these two things you will be very happy. You must
know that you are that which is not, but I am That Which Is.
If your soul is possessed of this knowledge . . . [y]ou will
never consent to anything which is against My commands.
Without difficulty you will attain all the gifts of grace and all
the virtues of love."

Acts 4:32–37
Psalm 93
John 3:7b–15

Whoever lives the truth comes to the light, so that his works
may be clearly seen as done in God.
—JOHN 3:21

Conversion is a continual unveiling; layer after layer of
hardness of heart, self-denial, and our own petty illusions of
ourselves are removed piece by piece. This exposure is not to
humiliate us but to humble us and draw us into reality.

Acts 5:17–26
Psalm 34
John 3:16–21

Thursday

MAY 1

• ST. JOSEPH THE WORKER •

For the one whom God sent speaks the words of God. He does
not ration his gift of the Spirit.
—JOHN 3:34

There is no allotted, measured portion of the Holy Spirit to
be received. Rather, the capacity to receive the Holy Spirit is
dictated by our own limitations, the obstacles we put in
place. God will never force his grace upon us. Furthermore,
we may severely limit ourselves in the capacity to receive
grace by our willfulness, sin, fear, or doubt.

Acts 5:27–33
Psalm 34
John 3:31–36
Or, for the Memorial
Genesis 1:26—2:3 or
Colossians 3:14–15, 17, 23–24
Matthew 13:54–58

Friday

MAY 2

"If this endeavor or this activity is of human origin, it will destroy itself. But if it comes from God, you will not be able to destroy them."
—ACTS 5:38–39

The Pharisee had this point correct: any endeavor that comes from God cannot be destroyed. When we are tempted to overestimate our own responsibility in outcomes, we need to remember whose work it is.

Acts 5:34–42
Psalm 27
John 6:1–15

• ST. PHILIP AND ST. JAMES, APOSTLES •

*Jesus said to him, "Have I been with you for so long a time and
you still do not know me, Philip?"*
—JOHN 14:9

Sometimes it helps to remember that many of our holiest,
most faithful brethren struggled to believe. The path to
sainthood is often marked by periods of doubt and
uncertainty. If we struggle in this arena, we know we are in
good company, and we can ask the special intercession of
those who have gone before us on the path to sanctity.

1 Corinthians 15:1–8
Psalm 19
John 14:6–14

He was made known to them in the breaking of the bread.
—LUKE 24:35

What Jesus reveals in the breaking of the bread—this is my
Body given for you—is that his entire being is directed
toward perfect love—making a gift of oneself. Do I make
Jesus known to the world in the same way? Is my life ordered
toward self-giving love? If not, why not?

Acts 2:14, 22–33
Psalm 16
1 Peter 1:17–21
Luke 24:13–35

Monday

MAY 5

"Do not work for food that perishes but for the food that endures for eternal life."
—JOHN 6:27

For fifty-plus years, my parents have prayed the Morning Offering together: "O Jesus, through the Immaculate Heart of Mary, I offer You my prayers, works, joys and sufferings of this day for all the intentions of Your Sacred Heart, in union with the Holy Sacrifice of the Mass throughout the world, in reparation for my sins, for the intentions of all my relatives and friends, and in particular for the intentions of the Holy Father. Amen." Jesus is not asking us to abandon earthly life; rather he is inviting us to bring him into every moment of it.

Acts 6:8–15
Psalm 119
John 6:22–29

Tuesday

MAY 6

Into your hands I commend my spirit.
—PSALM 31:6

When we commend ourselves, we ask that someone
remember us with kindness; we entrust ourselves to them.
When we've done all we know to do and exhausted our
options or abilities, we can commend ourselves to God, just
as the psalmist did, just as St. Stephen did in today's first
reading, just as Christ does on the cross.

Remember me kindly, O Lord.

Acts 7:51—8:1a
Psalm 31
John 6:30–35

Wednesday

MAY 7

Those who had been scattered went about preaching the word. . . . and many . . . people were cured. There was great joy in that city.
—ACTS 8:4, 7–8

It's easy to panic when we look at the evil around us. We might feel understaffed for the task at hand: the new evangelization. But these early accounts in Acts teach us that we must simply be about our work. Never mind that we may feel scattered and ineffectual. We go about our Father's business, and what follows? Conversion, healing, and great joy.

Acts 8:1b–8
Psalm 66
John 6:35–40

Thursday

MAY 8

He has given life to our souls.
—PSALM 66:9

The Eucharist, says the *Catechism*, is "the source and summit" of our faith—it is the primary way in which Christ has chosen to reveal himself to us. We want to receive the Eucharist well and often. But if we can't, we can still make a "spiritual communion," as St. John Vianney says. "When we cannot go to the church, let us turn towards the tabernacle; no wall can shut us out from the good God." This "living bread that came down from heaven" is life for our souls.

Acts 8:26–40
Psalm 66
John 6:44–51

"For my Flesh is true food, and my Blood is true drink. Whoever eats my Flesh and drinks my Blood remains in me and I in him."
—JOHN 6:55–56

If you're wondering where Jesus is, look to the Eucharist. If you're confused and don't know what to do, take your question to Jesus in the Eucharist. If you're in pain, lonely, starving for any crumb of tenderness or affection, go to Jesus, who is true food, true drink. If you want to say thank you for special graces and blessings, remain in Jesus in the Eucharist.

Acts 9:1–20
Psalm 117
John 6:52–59

"The words I have spoken to you are Spirit and life. But there are some of you who do not believe." Jesus knew from the beginning the ones who would not believe.
—JOHN 6:63–64

It may be that you live amidst unbelievers, even in your own home. This may be a source of sorrow and tension. But we can take heart in the fact that Jesus knows those who do not believe; he knows them even in their hardness of heart. This in itself is a pathway to conversion. He is not as far from them as we might think.

Acts 9:31–42
Psalm 116
John 6:60–69

Beloved: If you are patient when you suffer for doing what is good, this is a grace before God. For to this you have been called, because Christ also suffered for you.
—1 PETER 2:20–21

Suffering in the life of a Christian is a great paradox. We know that some of the saints even prayed for more suffering; they understood it so profoundly as a means to sanctification and greater grace. We may not be ready to go quite that far. Today, whatever suffering comes, simply and quietly thank God for it. Thank God that it hurts, thank God for this mysterious grace. Then wait and see what happens.

Acts 2:14a, 36–41
Psalm 23
1 Peter 2:20b–25
John 10:1–10

• ST. NEREUS AND ST. ACHILLEUS, MARTYRS, ST. PANCRAS, MARTYR •

As a hind longs for the running waters,
so my soul longs for you, O God.
Athirst is my soul for God, the living God.
When shall I go and behold the face of God?
Send forth your light and your fidelity;
they shall lead me on
And bring me to your holy mountain,
to your dwelling-place.
—PSALM 42:2–3; 43:3

May my desire for you, O Jesus, become ever more ardent and earnest. Increase my yearning heart, that I may long for more and more of you to fill it.

Acts 11:1–18
Psalm 42, 43
John 10:11–18

[He] encouraged them all to remain faithful to the Lord in
firmness of heart.
—ACTS 11:23

What a lovely contrast to "hardness of heart" is "firmness of
heart." The Christian life is not anchored necessarily in a
"soft heart," a soft life, but a heart set, fixed on the way of
the Lord.

In what ways is my heart hardened, and in what ways is it set
firmly in the will of God?

Acts 11:19–26
Psalm 87
John 10:22–30

"It was not you who chose me, but I who chose you and appointed you to go and bear fruit that will remain, so that whatever you ask the Father in my name he may give you. This I command you: love one another."
—JOHN 15:16–17

Even in the task of daily loving one another, we can trust that we have been chosen and appointed to bear fruit that will last. God will provide what is needed to those he chooses and appoints. You will have what you need to do what God asks of you today.

Acts 1:15–17, 20–26
Psalm 113
John 15:9–17

From this man's descendants God, according to his promise, has brought to Israel a savior, Jesus.
—ACTS 13:23

God has a plan. And you are a vital part of it.

Lord, today I will examine my life in the context of the salvation story, and I will give thanks that I am part of something so magnificent, a plan for redemption and restoration that stretches forward and backward through all time, beyond time.

Acts 13:13–25
Psalm 89
John 13:16–20

Friday

MAY 16

We ourselves are proclaiming this good news to you that what God promised our fathers he has brought to fulfillment for us, their children, by raising up Jesus.
—ACTS 13:32–33

Blessed John Paul II's pontificate was marked by a call to fearlessness patterned after that of Jesus and the earliest disciples. He wrote, "This is no time to be ashamed of the Gospel. It is the time to preach it from the rooftops. Do not be afraid to break out of comfortable and routine modes of living in order to take up the challenge of making Christ known in the modern metropolis."

Lord, where have I grown too comfortable?

Acts 13:26–33
Psalm 2
John 14:1–6

Saturday

MAY 17

"Whoever has seen me has seen the Father."
—JOHN 14:9

"A man is a father not primarily because he acts like a father,"
writes Don Briel, "but because he participates in some sort of
larger reality and therefore gives us a place in a cosmic order
of meaning. A father is important because our relationship to
him is central in defining who we are as persons. . . .
Somehow, to call God our Father is to transform ourselves as
persons, and we need to understand the nature of the
conversion that is implied in hungering for—and even more,
in accepting—a father's love."

Acts 13:44–52
Psalm 98
John 14:7–14

Sunday

MAY 18

• FIFTH SUNDAY OF EASTER •

"Brothers, select from among you seven reputable men, filled
with the Spirit and wisdom, whom we shall appoint to [serve at
table], whereas we shall devote ourselves to prayer and to the
ministry of the word."
—ACTS 6:3–4

The Christian community needs a variety of gifts and
vocations, and we need to ask one another for help. Am I
ever tempted to imagine that my gifts are less important than
others, and therefore, I don't really need to participate in the
work of the Church? Do I ever imagine that I'm not really
needed? Or do I imagine that I have to do it all, that I cannot
ever ask others to step up and serve?

Acts 6:1–7
Psalm 33
1 Peter 2:4–9
John 14:1–12

Jesus said to his disciples, "Whoever has my commandments and observes them is the one who loves me. Whoever loves me will be loved by my Father, and I will love him and reveal myself to him."
—JOHN 14:21

Our relationship with God is marked by these ever-deepening stages of revelation. The commandments first reveal to us our great need for grace. To live holy, healthy, loving lives, we need a grace and firmness of heart that we simply cannot muster on our own. As we bring ourselves fully revealed to Jesus, he reveals more of himself—his power and ready desire to bring us to wholeness.

Acts 14:5–18
Psalm 115
John 14:21–26

Tuesday

MAY 20

• ST. BERNARDINE OF SIENA, PRIEST •

"Peace I leave with you; my peace I give to you."
—JOHN 14:27

Blessed Mother Teresa once said, "If we have no peace, it is
because we have forgotten that we belong to each other."
Yes, you belong to Jesus and he belongs to you.

Lord, let me walk through this day understanding that every
person I encounter is profoundly loved, wanted, and created
by you; we are your dearly beloved.

Acts 14:19–28
Psalm 145
John 14:27–31a

"Remain in me as I remain in you."
—JOHN 15:4

What exactly does it mean to remain in Jesus?

We remain with Christ when we study his word, when we receive the sacraments, when we spend time in prayer, and when we serve one another in love. We stay with Jesus when we forgive those who wrong us, when we help those who cannot help themselves, when we tend to the lonely, the sick, and the poor in our midst. We remain in him when we live in gratitude and hope.

Acts 15:1–6
Psalm 122
John 15:1–8

Thursday

MAY 22

"God, who knows the heart...."
—ACTS 15:8

So very much suffering enters the world when a person feels unknown, misunderstood, unappreciated, and forgotten. It may be the most profound need of the human spirit—to be known and loved.

God knows your heart, loves your heart, and can heal your heart. God can remove the weight of the world's indifference.

Acts 15:7–21
Psalm 96
John 15:9–11

Friday

MAY 23

My heart is steadfast, O God; my heart is steadfast.
—PSALM 57:8

Make this portion of the psalm your theme song for the next year. Take it with you wherever you go. Pull it out of your pocket and read it ten times a day. Put it up on your mirror. Scribble it on a bookmark or make it your screensaver. No matter what comes your way, meet it with this verse: my heart is steadfast, O Lord! Cling to it and pray with it. Then get back to me in a year to let me know how it went.

Acts 15:22–31
Psalm 57
John 15:12–17

Saturday

MAY 24

"If you belonged to the world, the world would love its own; but because you do not belong to the world, and I have chosen you out of the world, the world hates you."
—JOHN 15:19

What do you really love about your spouse, child, friend, parent, neighbor, teacher, co-worker, priest, sister, brother? Do you love them for their money or their generosity? For their looks or their beautiful, loving heart? We love one another for our eternal value and the timeless, holy traits that spring up in us. In this passage, we concentrate not on the hate of the world but on the love and communion of heaven.

Acts 16:1–10
Psalm 100
John 15:18–21

Sunday

MAY 25

• SIXTH SUNDAY OF EASTER •

"I will not leave you orphans. I will come to you."
—JOHN 14:18

An orphan may experience an acute sense of abandonment
and a unique kind of disorientation in the world. Jesus'
promise is protection against these devastating
consequences: abandonment, rejection, being forgotten and
without home or heritage.

Lord, give me your name that I may be one of your family.

Acts 8:5–8, 14–17
Psalm 66
1 Peter 3:15–18
John 14:15–21

*"I have told you this so that when their hour comes you may
remember that I told you."*
—JOHN 16:4

Has your hour come? Did it take you by surprise? If you are
suffering persecution for your faith, know that you are in the
company of great saints and martyrs. If you are suffering an
unexpected loss, illness, or setback, God can give you the
grace required to move through it in holiness.

Acts 16:11–15
Psalm 149
John 15:26—16:4a

Tuesday

MAY 27

• ST. AUGUSTINE OF CANTERBURY, BISHOP •

"It is better for you that I go."
—JOHN 16:7

How heartbroken and confused the apostles must have been. "Grief filled their hearts." The life of the spirit requires that we accept difficult and mysterious losses at times. They are somehow an important part of the greater story of redemption and salvation. We needn't fear them, but trust that God's plan has something bigger and more comprehensive in mind.

Acts 16:22–34
Psalm 138
John 16:5–11

"When he comes, the Spirit of truth, he will guide you to all truth."
—JOHN 16:13

St. Augustine's prayer to the Holy Spirit is especially helpful in revealing the Spirit's power: "Breathe in me, O Holy Spirit, that my thoughts may all be holy. Act in me, O Holy Spirit, that my work, too, may be holy. Draw my heart, O Holy Spirit, that I love but what is holy. Strengthen me, O Holy Spirit, to defend all that is holy. Guard me, then, O Holy Spirit, that I always may be holy. Amen."

Acts 17:15, 22—18:1
Psalm 148
John 16:12–15

"And behold, I am with you always, until the end of the age."
—MATTHEW 28:20

How do we account for radical human loneliness? How are
we to understand the words of Jesus in light of that sense of
isolation or persecution?

Jesus, where are you in my loneliness? Like the Blessed
Mother, I do not doubt your power nor your faithfulness.
Only this will I ask, "How is this possible?"

Acts 1:1–11
Psalm 47
Ephesians 1:17–23
Matthew 28:16–20

Friday

MAY 30

"No one will take your joy away from you."
—JOHN 16:22

Keep this promise of Jesus in your pocket. There is a
moment ahead for you in which your joy will be complete.
You can draw that joy into every moment. Even now, live in
that joy. Call to mind the promise of God, a promise that
exists outside of time. Enter the mystery that tells us Jesus is
completing our joy this very moment.

Acts 18:9–18
Psalm 47
John 16:20–23

≥ 181 ≤

*"Most blessed are you among women, and blessed is the fruit of
your womb."*
—LUKE 1:42

I once heard the Visitation described as the first Eucharistic
procession, the first time Jesus was taken out in hidden form
to the world to be adored. And in this deep mystery, he still
"hides"—in all creation, in the Holy Eucharist, and in
redeemed humanity.

Jesus, may I reverence you wherever you abide.

Zephaniah 3:14–18a or
Romans 12:9–16
Isaiah 12:2–3, 4, 5–6
Luke 1:39–56

Sunday

JUNE 1

• SEVENTH SUNDAY OF EASTER •

Of you my heart speaks.
—PSALM 27:8

You: patient, loving, forgiving, beautiful, gentle, incredibly
patient. Merciful, powerful, almighty, healing, unifying,
magnificent, magnanimous, and still more patient. Just, kind,
compassionate, slow to anger, faithful, unable to forget me,
unable to abandon me, unable to fail. You know no fear. You:
my resting place, my stronghold, home to my heart.

Acts 1:12–14
Psalm 27
1 Peter 4:13–16
John 17:1–11a

⋑ 183 ⋐

Monday

JUNE 2

• ST. MARCELLINUS AND ST. PETER, MARTYRS •

"In the world you will have trouble, but take courage, I have conquered the world."
—JOHN 16:33

Do you believe it? What would you do differently if you believed, right down to your bones, that Jesus has conquered the world and its troubles?

Lord, give me courage to see the world the way you do, to see it as it really is.

Acts 19:1–8
Psalm 68
John 16:29–33

Tuesday

JUNE 3

• ST. CHARLES LWANGA AND COMPANIONS, MARTYRS •

"I pray for them . . . for the ones you have given me."
—JOHN 17:9

Jesus has lifted your name before the Father. *You* have been remembered to the Father by the Son. You belong to them, they know you and attend to you.

Every hour on the hour today, stop and consider this extraordinary grace and reality.

Acts 20:17–27
Psalm 68
John 17:1–11a

Awesome in his sanctuary is God, the God of Israel;
he gives power and strength to his people.
—PSALM 68:36

You can spend an hour with Jesus anywhere at any time, but I
wonder why Scripture is filled with so much discussion of
the "sanctuary" and the Holy of holies. Perhaps there is a
particular gift God wants to give us in adoration, when we
take ourselves to the sanctuary, that place appointed and
prepared for his very presence in the Eucharist. In that
sanctuary we make the physical effort to search for him and
to keep him company in the tabernacle.

Acts 20:28–38
Psalm 68
John 17:11b–19

Thursday

JUNE 5

• ST. BONIFACE, BISHOP AND MARTYR •

" . . . so that they may all be one. . . ."
—JOHN 17:21

We pay particular attention to the passages in which, while praying, Jesus, "lifting his eyes to heaven," addresses his Father directly on our behalf. The anchor of his prayer is always our unity, that we may be "brought to perfection as one."

Lord, in what areas of my life do I sow discord? Where do I fracture the body of Christ? How can I help to build it up in unity and peace, to join in the very prayer of Christ?

Acts 22:30; 23:6–11
Psalm 16
John 17:20–26

⇒ 187 ⇐

Friday

JUNE 6

• ST. NORBERT, BISHOP •

"Follow me."
—JOHN 21:19

Are we like Peter, insistent that we love the Lord and would do whatever he asked? Are we like Peter, who runs away in fear when things get prickly? Are we like Peter, who leans into an even deeper, more painful conversion and goes singing to his martyrdom, filled with love for God and his children, filled with an abiding willingness to forgive and hope in others, and a peace that surpasses all understanding?

Lord, help me understand what you are asking of me when you say, "follow me."

Acts 25:13b–21
Psalm 103
John 21:15–19

The LORD is in his holy temple;
the LORD's throne is in heaven.
His eyes behold,
his searching glance is on mankind.
—PSALM 11:4

What will he see in me today? What sorrow or worry or gratitude? What question or fear? What joy or peace or faithfulness? What courage or weariness? What pain or holy affection?

Acts 28:16–20, 30–31
Psalm 11
John 21:20–25

Sunday

JUNE 8

• PENTECOST •

*The Spirit too comes to the aid of our weakness; for we do not
know how to pray as we ought, but the Spirit himself intercedes
with inexpressible groanings.*
—ROMANS 8:26

Something so holy and deep cannot be uttered. The cry of
the Spirit on your behalf moves through the veil between
heaven and earth and covers you and cloaks the earth,
undetected and perpetual. This Spirit holds you up, fortifies
you, and meets your weakness in perfect, holy strength.

VIGIL:
Genesis 11:1–9 or Exodus 19:3–8,
16–20 or Ezekiel 37:1–14 or Joel 3:1–5
Psalm 104
Romans 8:22–27
John 7:37–39

EXTENDED VIGIL:
Genesis 11:1–9
Exodus 19:3–8, 16–20
Ezekiel 37:1–14
Joel 3:1–5
Psalm 104
John 7:37–39

DAY:
Acts 2:1–11
Psalm 104
1 Corinthians 12:3–7, 12–13 or
Galatians 5:16–25
John 20:19–23 or John 15:26–27;
16:12–15

"Blessed are the poor in spirit. . . ."
—MATTHEW 5:3

The poor in spirit know how to rightly receive. Caryll Houselander says it this way: "The pride which wants to give but not to receive, which resents sympathy and is content with unrequited love, is terrible, because it is pride which frustrates Christ. Where would we be, poor human creatures, were it not that Christ pleads from every human life, a beggar with outstretched hands? In every one of us there is some lack which is Christ's need."

1 Kings 17:1–6
Psalm 121
Matthew 5:1–12

Jesus said to his disciples: "You are the salt of the earth. But if salt loses its taste, with what can it be seasoned?"
—MATTHEW 5:13

A very learned, eloquent man I knew used the expression "salt of the earth" as though it were a great insult, like calling someone plain, pedestrian, even simple-minded. I watched him as he poured salt over his meal of steak-frites that night and wondered about my own relationship to salt, about my own "saltiness."

Lord, let me be this kind of salt: a plain, simple, essential flavor for the world, one we cannot do without.

1 Kings 17:7–16
Psalm 4
Matthew 5:13–16

He . . . encouraged them all to remain faithful to the Lord in firmness of heart, for he was a good man, filled with the Holy Spirit and faith.
—ACTS 11:23–24

Do you want to become good, one whose faith inspires others? Become the kind of saint who encourages and exhorts others to remain faithful. Become one of those in the world whose living and lovely faith brings hope and joy. The world needs it.

St. Barnabas, pray for us.

Acts 11:21b–26; 13:1–3
Psalm 98
Matthew 5:17–19

Thursday

JUNE 12

You have visited the land and watered it;
greatly have you enriched it.
. . . Thus have you prepared the land;
drenching its furrows, breaking up its clods,
Softening it with showers,
blessing its yield.
—PSALM 65:10–11

A drought hung over the Midwest years ago, and as time
passed and no rains came, an ominous feeling swelled
throughout the community. Would the crops survive? What
if fire broke out? We hung on every promise of a cloud. Rain
is a powerful metaphor, of the relief of God's presence to a
soul gone dry. Today, we pray for those who thirst for the
showers of God.

1 Kings 18:41–46
Psalm 65
Matthew 5:20–26

Friday

JUNE 13

• ST. ANTHONY OF PADUA, PRIEST AND DOCTOR OF THE CHURCH •

"But I say to you, everyone who looks at a woman with lust has already committed adultery with her in his heart."
—MATTHEW 5:28

St. Anthony of Padua reminds us, "Anyone, then, who desires to live chastely in Christ Jesus, must flee not only the mouse of lust, but even from its very scent." Let's not concentrate on the act of lust but on any act—intended or not—that may invite lust. How do I put myself together? Do I carry myself in a modest way? Do I try to attract undue attention? Do I have custody of my eyes?

1 Kings 19:9a, 11–16
Psalm 27
Matthew 5:27–32

"Let your 'Yes' mean 'Yes,' and your 'No' mean 'No.'"
—MATTHEW 5:37

Is Christ chastising us for being wishy-washy or uncertain?
Does he despise the confused or torn? Jesus is not opposed
to prudent deliberation, but once a decision has been made,
we need to stay the course unless we have good, substantial
reason to change it. We shouldn't be soft in our
commitments. A promise is a promise; a vow is a vow. The
world needs men and women who keep their word.

1 Kings 19:19–21
Psalm 16
Matthew 5:33–37

Brothers and sisters, rejoice. Mend your ways, encourage one another, agree with one another, live in peace, and the God of love and peace will be with you.
—2 CORINTHIANS 13:11

Live in peace, Paul says. What's one small thing you could do today in that direction? Encourage someone who is feeling low, refrain from correcting someone who is in the wrong? Is it really so important that you are right? Take one little action today to usher in the peace of God. And then do another one tomorrow, and the day after. Repeat until a habit of life is formed.

Exodus 34:4b–6, 8–9
Daniel 3:52, 53, 54, 55, 56
2 Corinthians 13:11–13
John 3:16–18

"Offer no resistance to one who is evil. When someone strikes you on your right cheek, turn the other one to him as well."
—MATTHEW 5:39

There's a difference between fighting for justice and exacting vengeance. Jesus isn't suggesting you become a doormat. Rather, he is asking for greater conversion of heart, where our energies are spent in proper order, not bent on protecting our vanity or pride, but inviting people into the love of truth, goodness, and beauty.

1 Kings 21:1–16
Psalm 5
Matthew 5:38–42

JUNE 17

"Pray for those who persecute you."
—MATTHEW 5:44

Forgiveness is often a process, and prayer is an important part of it. But it seems easier to forgive an offense that is over and done with than to continually forgive someone who is hurting us in a way that's ongoing and active. We can do as Jesus does, and ask God to forgive them for us—"Forgive them, they know not what they do." We trust that God can do for us what we cannot do for ourselves. We can step into the wake of his mercy.

1 Kings 21:17–29
Psalm 51
Matthew 5:43–48

"When you give alms, do not let your left hand know what your right is doing."
—MATTHEW 6:3

A spiritual director used to say that I needed to do one good turn for another person every single day without getting found out. Not getting found out is the hard part. When was the last time you did something for someone else in true anonymity and in true charity? See how many days in a row you can help someone without getting found out.

2 Kings 2:1, 6–14
Psalm 31
Matthew 6:1–6, 16–18

JUNE 19

• ST. ROMUALD, ABBOT •

Thy Kingdom come, thy will be done.
—MATTHEW 6:10

"Homecoming" by Ronda Chervin reflects on this clause of
the Our Father:

from glory in the whole
to piecework in my niche?
from contemplation to action?
descent from heaven?
No, lifting up the earth—
"Thy kingdom come."
Yes, my god, my Lord, My Father
I exult in being a woman of the kingdom.
Yes, my God, My Lord, My Father
I know that your kingdom is coming
Where the father will dance

Sirach 48:1–14
Psalm 97
Matthew 6:7–15

*"The lamp of the body is the eye. If your eye is sound, your
whole body will be filled with light."*
—MATTHEW 6:22

Do you spend more time looking at a screen than looking
into the eyes of others? Think about this today when you sit
in front of any computer, phone, or television. How is visual
technology affecting your spiritual life? Is it aiding you or
controlling you? What are you taking in, and how is it
affecting the way you see, encounter, and interact with
the world?

2 Kings 11:1–4, 9–18, 20
Psalm 132
Matthew 6:19–23

Do not worry about tomorrow; tomorrow will take care of itself.
—MATTHEW 6:34

Peter Kreeft makes a compelling argument that all fear is fear of the future. He writes in *Heaven: The Heart's Deepest Longing*, "Time is the condition for all fear; that's why time is the enemy. For fear is always of the future, fear of what might happen next, not of what is actually happening now. Some psychologists think as much as nine-tenths of pain is mental, not physical, induced by fear and removable by fearlessness."

2 Chronicles 24:17–25
Psalm 89
Matthew 6:24–34

Sunday

JUNE 22

• THE MOST HOLY BODY AND BLOOD OF CHRIST (CORPUS CHRISTI) •

*He therefore let you be afflicted with hunger, and then fed you
with manna, a food unknown to you and your fathers, in order
to show you that not by bread alone does one live, but by every
word that comes forth from the mouth of the LORD.*
—DEUTERONOMY 8:3

Affliction is allowed but met by an unknown "cure." Is there
some provision God is offering that you have not yet
recognized?

We pray for hearts that are open to your creative and
mysterious provisions, Lord. We pray for hearts that trust in
your word long before provisions arrive.

Deuteronomy 8:2–3, 14b–16a
Psalm 147
1 Corinthians 10:16–17
John 6:51–58

Monday

JUNE 23

Jesus said to his disciples: "Stop judging, that you may not be judged."
—MATTHEW 7:1

Catherine of Siena said that judgment was often the most pernicious vice and the last sin to leave us. "Whenever you think God has shown you other people's faults, take care," she cautions. "Your own judgment may well be at fault. Say nothing. And if you do attribute any vice to another person, immediately and humbly look for it in yourself also. Should the other person really possess that vice, he will correct himself so much the better when he sees how gently you understand him."

2 Kings 17:5–8, 13–15a, 18
Psalm 60
Matthew 7:1–5

⇒ 205 ⇐

Then the LORD extended his hand and touched my mouth,
saying,
See I place my words in your mouth!
This day I set you over nations and over kingdoms,
to root up and to tear down,
to destroy and to demolish,
to build and to plant.
—JEREMIAH 1:9–10

Before he became Pope Benedict XVI, Cardinal Joseph Ratzinger wrote that the person "comes in the profoundest sense to himself not through what he does but through what he accepts," not through what he achieves but through what he receives. John the Baptist did not create his prophetic gift; he received it and was able to achieve all that God asked of him.

VIGIL:	DAY:
Jeremiah 1:4–10	Isaiah 49:1–6
Psalm 71	Psalm 139
1 Peter 1:8–12	Acts 13:22–26
Luke 1:5–17	Luke 1:57–66, 80

The king made a covenant before the LORD that they would
follow him and observe his ordinances, statutes and decrees
with their whole hearts and souls, thus reviving the terms of the
covenant which were written in this book. And all the people
stood as participants in the covenant.
—2 KINGS 23:3

Our leaders go before us striking agreements, making
covenants, establishing laws and decrees, aligning our
countries and communities with either good or ill. Our
leaders help create the moral fabric of our society. Are we
responsible about whom we put in office? Do we pray
faithfully for those who serve the Church and our
government? Do we do what we can to support leaders who
are committed to defending those who cannot defend
themselves?

2 Kings 22:8–13; 23:1–3
Psalm 119
Matthew 7:15–20

*"Everyone who listens to these words of mine and acts on them
will be like a wise man who built his house on rock. The rain
fell, the floods came, and the winds blew and buffeted the
house. But it did not collapse; it had been set solidly on rock."*
—MATTHEW 7:24–25

Is your soul set on a solid foundation, or are you feeling on
the verge of collapse? The will of the Father places us on
firm ground. This doesn't mean that the rain of hardship will
never fall on us or that floods of despair may not
occasionally rise up against us. But if we earnestly seek the
Father's will, they will never destroy us, only strengthen and
prove us.

2 Kings 24:8–17
Psalm 79
Matthew 7:21–29

Friday

JUNE 27

"Come to me, all you who labor and are burdened, and I will give you rest. Take my yoke upon you and learn from me, for I am meek and humble of heart; and you will find rest for yourselves. For my yoke is easy, and my burden light."
—MATTHEW 11:28–30

Wouldn't it be a relief to really rest, free from the toil of pride and vanity, fear and anxiety, every earthly worry? Do you see, little one? Do you understand? The heart of Jesus invites you to rest, welcomes you to rest in him.

Rest.

Deuteronomy 7:6–11
Psalm 103
1 John 4:7–16
Matthew 11:25–30

Pour out your heart like water
in the presence of the LORD.
—LAMENTATIONS 2:19

The Lord's heart is not a teaspoon, not a cup, not a pool, or pond, or ocean. His heart is more vast than the universe and when I pour out my heart before him, he receives me completely. He doesn't miss a drop.

Lamentations 2:2, 10–14, 18–19
Psalm 74
Luke 2:41–51

Sunday

JUNE 29

• ST. PETER AND ST. PAUL, APOSTLES •

*Peter thus was being kept in prison, but prayer by the Church
was fervently being made to God on his behalf.*
—ACTS 12:5

Soon enough, an angel would appear and tap him on the
shoulder, the chains would drop from his wrists, he would
pass one guard and then two, and an iron gate would open
"by itself."

There are many ways to be imprisoned: addiction, illness,
loneliness, pride, rejection, hopelessness, fear. Fervent prayer
is a means to miraculous rescue. The prayers of our friends
and loved ones, joined with our own, are powerful enough to
break any bondage.

VIGIL:
Acts 3:1–10
Psalm 19
Galatians 1:11–20
John 21:15–19

DAY:
Acts 12:1–11
Psalm 34
2 Timothy 4:6–8, 17–18
Matthew 16:13–19

Monday

JUNE 30

• THE FIRST HOLY MARTYRS OF THE CHURCH OF ROME •

Beware, I will crush you into the ground
as a wagon crushes when laden with sheaves.
Flight shall perish from the swift,
and the strong man shall not retain his strength;
The warrior shall not save his life,
nor the bowman stand his ground;
The swift of foot shall not escape,
nor the horseman save his life.
And the most stouthearted of warriors
shall flee naked on that day, says the LORD.
—AMOS 2:13–16

In honor of the martyrs, we remember the strength of the
Lord, who judges and defends, the Lord who judges justly
the crimes of humanity, the Lord who remembers those who
have died for love of his name.

Amos 2:6–10, 13–16
Psalm 50
Matthew 8:18–22

At dawn I bring my plea expectantly before you.
—PSALM 5:4

A young mother I know struggles to keep a consistent prayer
life and feels guilty that she doesn't often pray first thing in
the morning. But when Scripture speaks of prayer at dawn,
it's important to think of it not just in terms of the time of
day, but also as a disposition of the heart. Our earliest
inclination in any need is to take it to Jesus. Before we have a
chance to let in any other thought, we turn first to God in
confidence.

Amos 3:1–8; 4:11–12
Psalm 5
Matthew 8:23–27

"Have you come here to torment us?"
—MATTHEW 8:29

Evil cannot withstand the presence of the good but is tormented by it. In the company of the true, the good, and the beautiful, evil will not sit silent. It will cry out, writhe in agony, and make itself known. Jesus was unafraid of these demons, and neither should we be frightened when confronted with evil. Jesus does not torment, but his presence and purity will come under attack from those who cannot withstand it.

Amos 5:14–15, 21–24
Psalm 50
Matthew 8:28–34

Thursday

JULY 3

• ST. THOMAS, APOSTLE •

"My Lord and my God!"
—JOHN 20:28

St. Thomas is remembered for his doubt, but we should not forget his pursuit of the truth. He does not give up easily. And neither does Jesus give up on him.

Lord, give us courage and persistence so that even when we doubt, we do not give up pursuing the truth. May we trust that you never give up pursuing us.

Ephesians 2:19–22
Psalm 117
John 20:24–29

Friday

JULY 4

• INDEPENDENCE DAY •

Behold, I long for your precepts;
in your justice give me life.
—PSALM 119:40

Independence is only worth having if it is achieved through justice, and only if it understands that independence does not truly exist outside of interdependence. Independence gives life only when we acknowledge that within "independence" is "dependence"—dependence on God our Creator and Sustainer, our source of all goodness and life.

Amos 8:4–6, 9–12
Psalm 119
Matthew 9:9–13

Saturday

JULY 5

"People do not put new wine into old wineskins. Otherwise the skins burst, the wine spills out, and the skins are ruined. Rather, they pour new wine into fresh wineskins, and both are preserved."
—MATTHEW 9:17

Old brittle wineskins would burst with the gas given off by new wine. Wineskins needed to be pliable enough to expand. The Kingdom of God is like new wine; it will require that our hearts expand. Jesus asks us to love our enemies and to pray for those who persecute us. He makes everything new, and this newness cannot be accommodated by a brittle, inflexible heart.

Amos 9:11–15
Psalm 85
Matthew 9:14–17

We are not debtors to the flesh, to live according to the flesh.
For if you live according to the flesh, you will die, but if by the
Spirit you put to death the deeds of the body, you will live.
—ROMANS 8:12–13

A young newlywed has just learned that her husband is
addicted to pornography. He had unwittingly hoped that
marriage would "cure him." Addiction of this kind is
especially insidious and difficult to overcome. The desires of
the body are natural and powerful, and this is probably why
the devil spends so much time trying to pervert this area
of life.

Today, we pray for all those who struggle with any form of
sexual addiction.

Zechariah 9:9–10
Psalm 145
Romans 8:9, 11–13
Matthew 11:25–30

Monday

JULY 7

Thus says the LORD: I will allure her;
I will lead her into the desert
and speak to her heart. . . .

She shall call me "My husband".
—HOSEA 2:16, 18

A child does not choose his mother's womb, but we do choose our lovers. The marriage bond is the most intimate there is because you share your whole person with your spouse; you become one flesh in a willing act of loving surrender and deep and holy desire. Every heart longs to be spoken to in this way, to be desired, chosen entirely. This is one of the reasons the image is so powerful and prominent in Holy Scripture.

Hosea 2:16, 17b–18, 21–22
Psalm 145
Matthew 9:18–26

Tuesday

JULY 8

The harvest is abundant but the laborers are few; so ask the master of the harvest to send out laborers for his harvest.
—MATTHEW 9:37–38

You are harvest; you are also laborer.

Lord, let me live today in this reality; each person I encounter is someone you love and want to bring home to your heart.

Hosea 8:4–7, 11–13
Psalm 115
Matthew 9:32–38

Look to the LORD in his strength;
seek to serve him constantly.
—PSALM 105:4

At first, Sr. Agnes lost the ability to stand, so she would sit in the dirt and pull weeds. When sitting outside became too painful, she sat in a soft chair and read to another sister who was blind. When sitting became too painful and she was bound to her bed, she recited the Scriptures she'd memorized aloud and told the other sisters stories to make them laugh. When she got too weak to talk, her fingers gently moved over her rosary beads. When she died, her gentle, quiet life of service lived on in those she served.

Hosea 10:1–3, 7–8, 12
Psalm 105
Matthew 10:1–7

I drew them with human cords,
with bands of love;
I fostered them like one
who raises an infant to his cheeks.
—HOSEA 11:4

My godson, Gabe, is all cheeks and chubbiness and loves to
be kissed. If you kiss his cheek and then withdraw, he will
toss his little face toward yours until you kiss him again. And
when you do, he smiles and laughs with absolute abandon
and delight. Who could resist him? Neither can we resist the
kiss of Jesus; his tender embrace and gentle affection bring
deep abandonment and delight. Lean into him; he will draw
you to him in love.

Hosea 11:1–4, 8c–9
Psalm 80
Matthew 10:7–15

Friday

JULY 11

• ST. BENEDICT, ABBOT •

Behold, you are pleased with sincerity of heart,
and in my inmost being you teach me wisdom.
—PSALM 51:8

Interiority: wisdom, sincerity of heart—these things sit at the
center of our being, hidden, protected, and cultivated in
quiet, private ways. These things the Lord values most. We
push against our culture that wants to expose too much—put
it all on television for the world to see—when we seek to
cultivate a private, interior world from which to live and
breathe.

Hosea 14:2–10
Psalm 51
Matthew 10:16–23

"Therefore do not be afraid of them. Nothing is concealed that
will not be revealed, nor secret that will not be known."
—MATTHEW 10:26

Revelation—our being revealed in a way proper to our
humanity, even though this might be painful for us—is
nothing to be feared. Bringing our lives into the light in
reconciliation is acknowledging reality and the truth of
things. We grow properly, flourishing in heart, when we are
rooted in the reality of heaven.

Isaiah 6:1–8
Psalm 93
Matthew 10:24–33

Sunday

JULY 13

My word shall not return to me void,
but shall do my will,
achieving the end for which I sent it.
—ISAIAH 55:11

In part this is why we spend so much time with God's word;
we need constantly to refresh our minds with remembrance
of what is coming to pass. God's kingdom comes: in the
sacraments, the holy Mass, in acts of charity and mercy, in
our turning away from sin. It comes in you and me as we lead
sacramental, holy lives. That is the end for which we are
created: eternal life with God.

Lord, do I help bring your word to fruition?

Isaiah 55:10–11
Psalm 65
Romans 8:18–23
Matthew 13:1–23 or 13:1–9

"Whoever finds his life will lose it, and whoever loses his life for my sake will find it."
—MATTHEW 10:39

Jesus, these paradoxes test my heart. They press into my willfulness and the part of my mind that wants things to add up neatly. Your mysteries challenge me, Lord, beyond what I can comprehend or bear. Show me how to embrace this mysterious life of loss and gain that you offer, this mystery of redemption and resurrection and healing, this life that never ends.

Isaiah 1:10–17
Psalm 50
Matthew 10:34—11:1

Tuesday

JULY 15

Great is the LORD and wholly to be praised
in the city of our God.
His holy mountain, fairest of heights,
is the joy of all the earth.
—PSALM 48:2–3

St. Bonaventure said it this way: "If there is anyone who is not enlightened by this sublime magnificence of created things, he is blind. If there is anyone who, seeing all these works of God, does not praise Him, he is dumb; if there is anyone who, from so many signs, cannot perceive God, that man is foolish."

Isaiah 7:1–9
Psalm 48
Matthew 11:20–24

The LORD will not cast off his people.
—PSALM 94:14

The great Carmelite, St. Therese of the Child Jesus, reminds us that "We can never have too much confidence in the good God who is so powerful and so merciful. We obtain from him as much as we hope for."

Jehovah, grow my capacity to hope in you.

Isaiah 10:5–7, 13b–16
Psalm 94
Matthew 11:25–27

Thursday

JULY 17

"Come to me, all you who labor and are burdened, and I will give you rest. Take my yoke upon you and learn from me, for I am meek and humble of heart; and you will find rest for yourselves."
—MATTHEW 11:28–29

Rest comes to the meek and humble because rest of spirit resides in humility and gentleness. What's one small bit of chaos you could resist today to rest with Jesus? What's one area of your life where you could say, "I can't do it all," and just let it go with humility and acceptance? What's one area of your life that sucks away your energy? Where could you make your life softer and meeker?

Isaiah 26:7–9, 12, 16–19
Psalm 102
Matthew 11:28–30

"I desire mercy, not sacrifice."
—MATTHEW 12:7

Jesus draws from the prophet Hosea. When he quotes the Old Testament, it's often to show that he is the fulfillment of its promise. This is a radical shift—from fulfillment of the law of justice to fulfillment of the law of love. It is fulfilled with Christ's passion, death, and resurrection, and it brings a mysterious completion to God's plan for and presence among his people.

Isaiah 38:1–6, 21–22, 7–8
Isaiah 38:10, 11, 12abcd, 16
Matthew 12:1–8

You do see, for you behold misery and sorrow,
taking them in your hands.
—PSALM 10:14

Concentrate on the greatest source of misery or sorrow in
your life. What is it? A broken relationship or prolonged
unemployment? Temptation? Neglect? Loneliness? Boredom?
A sense of failure or uselessness? Illness? Whatever it is, let it
take shape in your mind and heart. Then, imagine Jesus
sitting before you, calm and strong. He stretches out his
open palms to you, and into them you place this thing, this
torment, this misery, this sorrow. After you've given it
completely into his hands, what does Jesus do with it?

Micah 2:1–5
Psalm 10
Matthew 12:14–21

Sunday

July 20

*You gave your children good ground for hope
that you would permit repentance for their sins.*
—Wisdom 12:19

When I faced a particularly protracted problem, my mom
bought me a magnet for my refrigerator which read, "It's
never too late." Indeed, no matter what I've done, no matter
how much time has passed, no matter how much I've
struggled and fallen and failed, I have formidable,
unshakeable, eternal reason to hope in God's mercy and
forgiveness. God is more interested in my repentant
heart—whatever it takes—than in my preferred timing
and comfort.

Wisdom 12:13, 16–19
Psalm 86
Romans 8:26–27
Matthew 13:24–43 or 13:24–30

You have been told, O man, what is good,
and what the LORD requires of you:
Only to do the right and to love goodness,
and to walk humbly with your God.
—MICAH 6:8

Truth, goodness, and beauty bear rationality and an ease of
spirit; unless we are wildly disordered, something in us
knows "the right" when we see it. But we tend to complicate
things, want to talk ourselves out of the good and pretend it's
impossible for us to choose, or that the sacrifices necessary
in choosing are just too great. Doing what's right isn't always
easy, but we can know the right thing—and love it and
choose to bring it about.

Micah 6:1–4, 6–8
Psalm 50
Matthew 12:38–42

Tuesday

JULY 22

• ST. MARY MAGDALENE •

Whoever is in Christ is a new creation: the old things have passed away; behold, new things have come.
—2 CORINTHIANS 5:17

No one knew better than Mary Magdalene that in Christ we are made new; she knew it body and soul. Saints like Mary Magdalene remind us just how far God will go to save us. None of us is out of his reach. We can all be made new.

St. Mary Magdalene, pray for us.

2 Corinthians 5:14–17
Psalm 63
John 20:1–2, 11–18

⇒ 234 ⇐

JULY 23

• ST. BRIDGET OF SWEDEN, RELIGIOUS •

Have no fear before them,
because I am with you to deliver you,
says the LORD.
Then the LORD extended his hand and touched my mouth,
saying,
See, I place my words in your mouth!
—JEREMIAH 1:8–9

Jeremiah was frightened that he was unprepared for the task God had given him. Ever feel like that—not enough? Not virtuous enough or courageous enough or smart enough? We are given challenging appointments to speak for the poor, to protect the vulnerable, to demand justice and religious freedom. It's not easy; we are not enough. But the Lord is, and he will touch us and give us what we need—words, strength, courage, faith, hope, tenacious love.

Jeremiah 1:1, 4–10
Psalm 71
Matthew 13:1–9

Thursday
JULY 24

"They look but do not see and hear but do not listen or understand."
—MATTHEW 13:13

The price of seeing, hearing, and understanding is conversion. Am I willing to change? To be more deeply converted? It is a choice I make, a movement of the will in which I participate. Isaiah said, "Gross is the heart of this people, they will hardly hear with their ears, they have closed their eyes, lest they see with their eyes and hear with their ears and understand with their hearts and be converted and I heal them."

Jesus, I ask for the courage to be truly converted and healed.

Jeremiah 2:1–3, 7–8, 12–13
Psalm 36
Matthew 13:10–17

*The grace bestowed in abundance on more and more people
may cause the thanksgiving to overflow for the glory of God.*
—2 CORINTHIANS 4:15

One way to determine if you're really doing God's work is to
examine your life for this character of
"moreness"—abundance and overflow, surplus and plenty.
God's moving through the world with more grace than you
even knew you needed, more grace to do more than you ever
dreamed you'd be capable of doing. More of God's presence
and power and divine operation.

2 Corinthians 4:7–15
Psalm 126
Matthew 20:20–28

Saturday

JULY 26

• ST. JOACHIM AND ST. ANNE, PARENTS OF THE BLESSED VIRGIN MARY •

"Blessed are your eyes, because they see, and your ears, because they hear."
—MATTHEW 13:16

Sts. Joachim and Anne are good reminders that we are part of a much larger story. Their faithful and largely anonymous lives played a critically important role in salvation history. An anonymous and faithful life may be exactly what God calls you to, as well, and it may be precisely because of its "smallness" that it will play such a great part in saving souls.

Lord, am I daring enough to see, to hear, to live a quiet, holy, and hidden life?

Sirach 44:1, 10–15
Psalm 132
Matthew 13:16–17

Sunday

JULY 27

*"Give your servant, therefore, an understanding heart to judge
your people and to distinguish right from wrong"* . . .

The LORD was pleased that Solomon made this request.

—1 KINGS 3:9–10

Are my requests pleasing to the Lord? What virtue do I need
to grow if I am to live out my vocation well? Patience, hope,
fidelity, wisdom, moral courage, perseverance?

Lord, let my prayers be pleasing to you.

1 Kings 3:5, 7–12
Psalm 119
Romans 8:28–30
Matthew 13:44–52 or 13:44–46

You were unmindful of the Rock that begot you,
You forgot the God who gave you birth.
—DEUTERONOMY 32:18

Does this describe someone you know? Is there someone
near you who has forgotten the mysterious reality of his or
her creation? Has this person fallen into despair, thinking her
life meaningless? Has he gone the other direction and
become arrogant, thinking himself master of his own fate?
The consequences of forgetting our origins are dire, not just
for us, but for everyone.

Jeremiah 13:1–11
Deuteronomy 32:18–19, 20, 21
Matthew 13:31–35

*"Martha, Martha, you are anxious and worried about many
things. There is need of only one thing."*
—LUKE 10:41–42

Poor Martha, ever remembered as a worrywart with poor
priorities. But someone had to serve the meal, right? Two
things to note: one, Martha had a strong sense of justice. It
wasn't necessarily wrong to point out how she felt
abandoned to do the work alone. She was thinking, no
doubt, of the comfort of her guests. And two, Jesus reminds
us that there is a higher order at work. In his presence, the
normal rules may not apply or may be rewritten altogether.

1 John 4:7–16
Psalm 34
John 11:19–27 or Luke 10:38–42

Wednesday

JULY 30

• ST. PETER CHRYSOLOGUS, BISHOP AND DOCTOR OF THE CHURCH •

O, my strength!
—PSALM 59:18

Strength and weakness are funny things in the life of the
spirit. St. Peter Chrysologus wrote, "Mildness overcomes
anger, meekness extinguishes fury . . . patience is the scourge
of impatience, gentle words vanquish quarrelsomeness, and
humility prostrates pride."

Jeremiah 15:10, 16–21
Psalm 59
Matthew 13:44–46

Thursday

JULY 31

Like clay in the hand of the potter, so are you in my hand.
—JEREMIAH 18:6

Wounded in battle, Ignatius begrudgingly read stories of the saints as he recovered. But he found the stories deeply engaging and soon began dreaming of becoming a "knight for Christ." So might we all be so perfectly re-formed. He wrote, "Few souls understand what God would accomplish in them if they were to abandon themselves unreservedly to Him and if they were to allow His grace to mold them accordingly."

Jesus, mold me according to your plan for my life.

Jeremiah 18:1–6
Psalm 146
Matthew 13:47–53

And they took offense at him.
—MATTHEW 13:57

The Church has always been a sign of contradiction; there
will always be those who are offended by her—just as they
were offended by Jesus. "The Church is a mystery," writes
Henri de Lubac, "that is to say . . . she is herself the great
sacrament that contains and vitalizes all others. In this world
she is the sacrament of Christ, as Christ himself, in his
humanity is for us the sacrament of God."

Jeremiah 26:1–9
Psalm 69
Matthew 13:54–58

Saturday

AUGUST 2

• ST. EUSEBIUS OF VERCELLI, BISHOP •

But I am afflicted and in pain;
let your saving help, O God, protect me.
—PSALM 69:30

Pain—whether physical, spiritual, or emotional—can be transforming or deforming. Today, let's offer whatever pain we may bear to God and ask him to redeem it and make it transformative. Today, let's also remember those who suffer chronic pain.

We ask, O Lord, that you remember your children who suffer great pain today, and we ask to take a little of their pain on ourselves, that theirs may be greatly alleviated by our communal intercession.

Jeremiah 26:11–16, 24
Psalm 69
Matthew 14:1–12

Sunday

AUGUST 3

All you who are thirsty,
come to the water!
You who have no money,
come, receive grain and eat;
Come, without paying and without cost,
drink wine and milk!
—ISAIAH 55:1

We pay special attention to the images of feasts and food in
Scripture. "The people of the first century," write the authors
of *The Food and Feasts of Jesus*, "instinctively understood
something about the experience of dining that we seem to
have forgotten. Common meals forge community. The act of
dining together creates a bond between those at the meal."
And the invitation we receive here in Isaiah creates a
community of eternal company as pure gift.

Isaiah 55:1–3
Psalm 145
Romans 8:35, 37–39
Matthew 14:13–21

*When . . . you have warned a virtuous man not to sin, and he
has in fact not sinned, he shall surely live because of the
warning, and you shall save your own life.*
—EZEKIEL 3:21

St. John Vianney reminds us, "The priesthood is the love of
the heart of Jesus. When you see a priest, think of our Lord
Jesus Christ. . . . It is the priest who continues the work of
redemption here on earth. . . . What use would be a house
filled with gold, were there no one to open its door? The
priest holds the key . . . it is he who opens the door. . . . The
priest is not a priest for himself, he is a priest for you."

We pray for our priests.

Ezekiel 3:17–21
Psalm 117
Matthew 9:35—10:1

AUGUST 5

"Lord, if it is you," Peter replied, "Tell me to come to you on the water." "Come," he said. Then Peter got out of the boat and began to walk on the water toward Jesus.
—MATTHEW 14:28–29

Do you need courage to get out of the boat?

The love of Jesus soars above the laws of this world. It surrounds them, orders them according to his command. When Christ says, "Come," he will hold you. He will hold you up, safe and secure above any dark waters.

Jeremiah 30:1–2, 12–15, 18–22
Psalm 102
Matthew 14:22–36 or 15:1–2, 10–14

Wednesday

AUGUST 6

• THE TRANSFIGURATION OF THE LORD •

Thousands upon thousands were ministering to him,
and myriads upon myriads attended him.
—DANIEL 7:10

The Transfiguration reminds us of our communal reality.
When you serve the Lord on earth, you join the company of
his dazzling and holy attendants in heaven, thousands upon
thousands, myriads upon myriads. You do not strive alone in
your service to God; you are joined and supported and
attended by the seen and unseen—Moses and Elijah and all
the saints and angels. Heaven is populated with powerful
allies waiting and ready to help you; that's your reality.

Daniel 7:9–10, 13–14
Psalm 97
2 Peter 1:16–19
Matthew 17:1–9

⇒ 249 ⇐

Thursday

AUGUST 7

• ST. SIXTUS II, POPE AND MARTYR, AND COMPANIONS, MARTYRS •

The days are coming, says the LORD, when I will make a new
covenant with the house of Israel and the house of Judah. . . . I
will place my law within them, and write it upon their hearts; I
will be their God, and they shall be my people.
—JEREMIAH 31:31, 33

Jesus is the new covenant. He is the new law of love and
forgiveness, the covenant that makes it possible for me to
call God, Father. Jesus is the law written within my heart; I
belong to him and he has given himself for me.

Jeremiah 31:31–34
Psalm 51
Matthew 16:13–23

⇒250⇐

Friday

AUGUST 8

• ST. DOMINIC, PRIEST •

"What can one give in exchange for his life?"
—MATTHEW 16:26

This is the whole point of the Church's fight to protect human dignity from conception to natural death: no one has created himself or herself. Life is pure gift, pure grace. What would you give for yours?

Nahum 2:1, 3; 3:1–3, 6–7
Deuteronomy 32:35cd–36ab,
39abcd, 41
Matthew 16:24–28

Saturday

AUGUST 9

• ST. TERESA BENEDICTA OF THE CROSS, VIRGIN AND MARTYR •

"Amen, I say to you, if you have faith the size of a mustard seed, you will say to this mountain, 'Move from here to there,' and it will move. Nothing will be impossible for you."
—MATTHEW 17:20

Jesus rebukes his disciples for their "little faith," a faith that shrinks God into abstractions. St. Teresa reminds us that "the way of faith gives us more than the way of philosophical thought: it gives us God, near to us as a person, who loves us and deals with us mercifully, giving us that security which human knowledge cannot give. But the way of faith is dark."

St. Teresa, please pray for our illumination.

Habakkuk 1:12—2:4
Psalm 9
Matthew 17:14–20

Peter got out of the boat and began to walk on the water toward
Jesus. But when he saw how strong the wind was he became
frightened; and, beginning to sink, he cried out, "Lord, save me!"
—MATTHEW 14:29–30

How human—to measure the strong wind and become
frightened. We must not focus on our circumstances, no
matter how daunting or terrifying—but on our powerful,
saving God.

Today, I will make a list of the many prayers answered, the
examples of how God has saved me and my loved ones. And
when I am frightened, I will make a conscious effort to turn
my mind to God's saving power.

1 Kings 19:9a, 11–13a
Psalm 85
Romans 9:1–5
Matthew 14:22–33

Monday

AUGUST 11

• ST. CLARE, VIRGIN •

Praise the LORD from the heavens;
praise him in the heights.
Praise him, all you his angels;
praise him, all you his hosts.
Let the kings of the earth and all peoples,
the princes and all the judges of the earth,
Young men too, and maidens,
old men and boys.
Praise the name of the LORD,
for his name alone is exalted;
His majesty is above earth and heaven.
—PSALM 148:1–2, 11–13

St. Clare says it this way: "Totally love Him, Who gave
Himself totally for your love."

Ezekiel 1:2–5, 24–28c
Psalm 148
Matthew 17:22–27

⇒254⇐

AUGUST 12

• ST. JANE FRANCES DE CHANTAL, RELIGIOUS •

"It is not the will of your heavenly Father that one of these little ones be lost."
—MATTHEW 18:14

Wouldn't it be a relief to know that there is someone who'd go to any length to find you if you were lost? Someone whose whole attention would be fixed on your well-being?

No matter how long it takes, no matter how far you may have strayed, He will find you. And His joy in this will be beyond measure.

Ezekiel 2:8—3:4
Psalm 119
Matthew 18:1–5, 10, 12–14

• ST. PONTIAN, POPE AND MARTYR; ST. HIPPOLYTUS, PRIEST AND MARTYR •

"If your brother sins against you, go and tell him his fault between you and him alone . . . If he does not listen, take one or two others along with you, so that every fact may be established . . . If he refuses to listen to them, tell the Church. If he refuses the listen even to the Church, then treat him as you would a Gentile or a tax collector."
—MATTHEW 18:15–17

It's critically important not to skip step one. This one takes the most moral courage and much prayer.

Ezekiel 9:1–7; 10:18–22
Psalm 113
Matthew 18:15–20

Thursday

AUGUST 14

• ST. MAXIMILIAN MARY KOLBE, PRIEST AND MARTYR •

*"Lord, if my brother sins against me, how often must I
forgive him?"*
—MATTHEW 18:21

Martyred at Auschwitz, St. Maximilian offered his life in
place of another. As a child, he had a vision of the Blessed
Mother: "She came to me holding two crowns, one white,
the other red. She asked me if I was willing to accept either
of these crowns. The white one meant that I should
persevere in purity, and the red that I should become a
martyr. I said that I would accept them both." He was killed
August 14, 1941, and his remains cremated on August 15, the
Feast of the Assumption.

Ezekiel 12:1–12
Psalm 78
Matthew 18:21—19:1

Friday

AUGUST 15

The queen takes her place at your right hand.
—PSALM 45:10

In *Redemptoris Mater*, Blessed John Paul II writes that "her presence in the midst of Israel—a presence so discreet as to pass almost unnoticed by the eyes of her contemporaries—shone very clearly before the Eternal One, who had associated this hidden 'daughter of Sion' with the plan of salvation embracing the whole history of humanity." The Assumption reminds us that we are all part of the plan of salvation and will be brought to completion in Christ.

VIGIL:
1 Chronicles 15:3–4, 15–16; 16:1–2
Psalm 132
1 Corinthians 15:54b–57
Luke 11:27–28

DAY:
Revelation 11:19a; 12:1–6a, 10ab
Psalm 45
1 Corinthians 15:20–27
Luke 1:39–56

"Let the children come to me, and do not prevent them; for the Kingdom of heaven belongs to such as these."
—MATTHEW 19:14

Today, we pray for an end to abortion, child abuse and neglect, child labor and slavery, and other atrocities committed against children.

Ezekiel 18:1–10, 13b, 30–32
Psalm 51
Matthew 19:13–15

"O woman, great is your faith! Let it be done for you as you wish." And the woman's daughter was healed from that hour.
—MATTHEW 15:28

What does it mean that Jesus would initially withhold his healing grace from the Canaanite woman? Ancestry would have been of supreme importance to those in the crowd, but this is not a subtle racist or sexist commentary. Instead, Jesus makes clear that his message of grace and healing is available to all who genuinely seek his mercy. His pause points us toward faith.

Isaiah 56:1, 6–7
Psalm 67
Romans 11:13–15, 29–32
Matthew 15:21–28

"Teacher, what good must I do to gain eternal life?"
—MATTHEW 19:16

We all know the answer to this question: "Sell what you have
and come follow me." And the young man went away sad,
"for he had many possessions." Lord, would I go away sad?
What do I own that owns me? Where do I need to grow in
detachment, surrender, honesty, and willingness?

Ezekiel 24:15–24
Deuteronomy 32:18–19, 20, 21
Matthew 19:16–22

Tuesday

AUGUST 19

• ST. JOHN EUDES, PRIEST •

Thus says the LORD God:
Because you are haughty of heart
you say, "A god am I!"
—EZEKIEL 28:2

Every little act of willfulness, even the petty, mean thoughts
no one knows about but me—this is my heart saying,
"A god am I!"

Ezekiel 28:1–10
Deuteronomy 32:26–27ab, 27cd–28,
30, 35cd–36ab
Matthew 19:23–30

Wednesday

AUGUST 20

• ST. BERNARD, ABBOT AND DOCTOR OF THE CHURCH •

"Are you envious because I am generous?"
—MATTHEW 20:15

Envy is corrosive and like all sin, the one who suffers most is not the object of envy but the one who envies. At the bottom of every envious thought is some fear all dressed up in longing.

Lord, I bring you my longings. I entrust them to your plan for me. Make still my envious heart.

Ezekiel 34:1–11
Psalm 23
Matthew 20:1–16

Thursday

AUGUST 21

• ST. PIUS X, POPE •

*I will give you a new heart and place a new spirit within you,
taking from your bodies your stony hearts and giving you
natural hearts.*
—EZEKIEL 36:26

He'd walled himself off from the whole world—stone upon
stone, brick upon brick. What could get through it? One
day, and then another day, and still another, someone,
through the grace of Jesus, noticed him and loved him. The
lie that he was unlovable was gradually defeated. And bit by
bit, his stony heart was loved back into real and
pulsing flesh.

Love is what animates the heart and revives both spirit
and flesh.

Ezekiel 36:23–28
Psalm 51
Matthew 22:1–14

Friday

AUGUST 22

• THE QUEENSHIP OF THE BLESSED VIRGIN MARY •

I will put my spirit in you that you may live, and I will settle you
upon your land; thus you shall know that I am the LORD. I have
promised, and I will do it, says the LORD.
—EZEKIEL 37:14

Sun and more sun. A string of 100-degree days. Power out
and water scarce. Wilting trees and plants and crops and
hearts. Fire comes to burn up the parched earth, devouring
everything in a wicked hiss of flame. Nature speaks to our
spiritual condition. Lord—how we need you! Come quickly
and save us from this dry death.

Mary, Queen of Heaven, pray for us.

Ezekiel 37:1–14
Psalm 107
Matthew 22:34–40

All their works are performed to be seen.
—MATTHEW 23:5

Posing is very dangerous, as much as our culture seems to flourish on it. Our insides do not match our outsides, and whole industries cater to image management, whole economies built on the fear of what others think. We long to be seen—in a certain light. It's only human. But God sees the heart perfectly, and there is nothing hidden from him.

Jesus, let me concentrate on what you see. Make me humble enough to be authentic.

Ezekiel 43:1–7a
Psalm 85
Matthew 23:1–12

AUGUST 24

I will give thanks to you, O LORD, with all my heart,
for you have heard the words of my mouth.
—PSALM 138:1

Indeed, the longings of my heart are known to you; you do not spurn me, not even for a moment. Lord, you are generous, and your presence attends me all my days. There is no darkness from which you cannot rescue me, no loss you cannot restore, no sin you cannot redeem, no fallenness you cannot set aright. My heart is yours. Do with me as you will.

Isaiah 22:19–23
Psalm 138
Romans 11:33–36
Matthew 16:13–20

*"One who swears by the altar swears by it and all that is upon it;
one who swears by the temple swears by it and by him who
dwells in it; one who swears by heaven swears by the throne of
God and by him who is seated on it."*
—MATTHEW 23:20–22

Altar, temple, throne: holy concentric circles spiraling
toward heaven. A priest on retreat once said, "All we are, we
bring here," and he gestured to the altar. Yes, we bring all we
are to the altar and offer ourselves. We are sanctified by the
one who has gone before us to mediate and redeem, to give
us recourse to temple and throne, the very seat of heaven.

2 Thessalonians 1:1–5, 11–12
Psalm 96
Matthew 23:13–22

Tuesday

AUGUST 26

*May our Lord Jesus Christ himself and God our Father, who has
loved us and given us everlasting encouragement and good hope
through his grace, encourage your hearts and strengthen them
in every good deed and word.*
—2 THESSALONIANS 3:16

If nothing else, the epistles teach us that letter writing is a
lost art. Have you noted how they are filled with salutations
of blessing, thanksgiving, encouragement, and exhortation?
Write someone a letter today, someone who needs blessing,
encouragement, exhortation, or thanks. Write your own little
epistle of love and hope and grace. Use pen and paper; apply
heart and the Holy Spirit.

2 Thessalonians 2:1–3a, 14–17
Psalm 96
Matthew 23:23–26

⇒269⇐

You shall eat the fruit of your handiwork.
—PSALM 128:2

St. Monica is best known for her prayers on behalf of the
conversion of her son, Augustine, who would become a
doctor of the Church and one of the most important
theological minds and penetrating, revealing hearts of all
Christendom. When we don't know how to pray for one
another, it is enough simply to ask the Lord for his will and
for deeper conversion of heart. He will take care of the rest.

2 Thessalonians 3:6–10, 16–18
Psalm 128
Matthew 23:27–32

Thursday

AUGUST 28

• ST. AUGUSTINE, BISHOP AND DOCTOR OF THE CHURCH •

His greatness is unsearchable.
—PSALM 145:3

And yet, how Augustine searched for God. This conversion
story is notable for how diligently this fine mind sought the
truth. Augustine asks, "What is wisdom but the truth in
which the supreme good is discerned and grasped?" In his
Confessions, he writes, "The happy life is joy based on truth.
This is joy grounded in you, O God, who are the truth, my
illumination, the salvation of my face, my God."

St. Augustine, pray for us that we may seek the truth with
bold and brave hearts.

1 Corinthians 1:1–9
Psalm 145
Matthew 24:42–51

⇒ 271 ⇐

AUGUST 29

• BEHEADING OF ST. JOHN THE BAPTIST, MARTYR •

They will fight against you, but not prevail over you,
for I am with you to deliver you, says the LORD.
—JEREMIAH 1:19

How do we reconcile this promise with martyrdom? We
remember that martyrdom is fueled by love of God and that
God's grace enables the martyr to lovingly, even joyfully,
embrace death. We do not martyr ourselves out of pride or
our own strength; rather God gives us such grace that we fall
in love with truth and love it more than our earthly life.
Martyrdom is more about the right ordering of love than
about suffering and death.

Jeremiah 1:17–19
Psalm 71
Mark 6:17–29

AUGUST 30

"Well done, my good and faithful servant. Since you were faithful in small matters, I will give you great responsibilities."
—MATTHEW 25:21

My financial planner asks me if I am "risk-averse" when it comes to money. I tell her I am risk-averse in all things; I've always had a tendency to play it safe. But I know that love and faithfulness require a certain level of risk, a willingness to put my heart out there and trust that God will be with me no matter the outcome. God certainly does not ask me to be imprudent, but neither does he want me to sit passively.

1 Corinthians 1:26–31
Psalm 33
Matthew 25:14–30

*The word of the LORD has brought me
derision and reproach all the day.*

*I say to myself, I will not mention him,
I will speak in his name no more.
But then it becomes like fire burning in my heart,
imprisoned in my bones;
I grow weary holding it in, I cannot endure it.*
—JEREMIAH 20:8–9

Jeremiah's gift is prophecy—and it is costing him something
to use it. So he tries to stifle it but to no avail. When our
spiritual gifts are well-formed and trained, we cannot *not*
exercise them. We cannot contain them but must unleash
their power to serve others regardless of the cost—derision,
unpopularity, fatigue, suffering great or small.

Jeremiah 20:7–9
Psalm 63
Romans 12:1–2
Matthew 16:21–27

He unrolled the scroll and found the passage where it was
written:
"The Spirit of the LORD is upon me,
because he has anointed me
to bring glad tidings to the poor.
He has sent me to proclaim liberty to captives
and recovery of sight to the blind,
to let the oppressed go free,
and to proclaim a year acceptable to the LORD."
—LUKE 4:17–19

Jesus, I wonder what was going through your mind. Were you frightened to become who you were meant to be? Your calling was so mysteriously impossible. You made your declaration, and they hated you for it, chased you from town. Give me courage, Lord, to become who you are asking me to be.

1 Corinthians 2:1–5
Psalm 119
Luke 4:16–30

We have the mind of Christ.
—1 CORINTHIANS 2:16

"We have not received the spirit of the world, but the Spirit who is from God," said Paul. Conforming our minds to the mind of Christ is an exacting and ongoing work, but this is precisely what we are up to in the sacraments, in study of Scripture, in prayer and meditation. We are taking on Christ, his thoughts, his intentions, his work, his love, and his transforming power.

1 Corinthians 2:10b–16
Psalm 145
Luke 4:31–37

From his fixed throne he beholds
all who dwell on the earth,
He who fashioned the heart of each,
he who knows all their works.
—PSALM 33:14–15

St. Gregory exhorted us in this way: "Be not anxious about what you have, but about what you are."

Jesus, see my heart and perfect it.

1 Corinthians 3:1–9
Psalm 33
Luke 4:38–44

Let no one deceive himself. If anyone among you considers himself wise in this age, let him become a fool, so as to become wise. . . . "The Lord knows the thoughts of the wise, that they are vain."
—1 CORINTHIANS 3:18, 20

Charles Dickens wrote, "There is a wisdom of the head, and a wisdom of the heart." The Christian life calls us to inhabit both—faith and reason, heart and mind—in perfect synchronicity. We fall in love with the truth.

1 Corinthians 3:18–23
Psalm 24
Luke 5:1–11

He will bring to light what is hidden in darkness and will manifest the motives of our hearts.
—1 CORINTHIANS 4:5

I do not have to spend time examining or judging anyone else's motives, only my own.

1 Corinthians 4:1–5
Psalm 37
Luke 5:33–39

The LORD is near to all who call upon him,
to all who call upon him in truth.
He fulfills the desire of those who fear him,
he hears their cry and saves them.
—PSALM 145:18–19

The truth isn't always easy or tidy. Maybe the truth is we are feeling sorely tempted, we've committed some sin we cannot bring ourselves to confess, or maybe we're toying with committing some sin, talking ourselves into it. We can call on the Lord in truth; we can say, "Lord, I'm tempted, I'm lonely, I'm afraid, I have sinned and I need your forgiveness, I've ruined things and I don't know what to do."

1 Corinthians 4:6b–15
Psalm 145
Luke 6:1–5

SEPTEMBER 7

Love does no evil to the neighbor;
hence, love is the fulfillment of the law.
—ROMANS 13:10

What is the loving thing? To speak or stay silent? To pray or to act? To be still and wait or to press forward? To sleep or to spend one hour with you? Lord, show me the ways that I am to fulfill the law.

Ezekiel 33:7–9
Psalm 95
Romans 13:8–10
Matthew 18:15–20

"Do not be afraid to take Mary your wife into your home."
—MATTHEW 1:20

In some of the earliest artistic renderings of St. Joseph, he is
seen—not adoring the Christ child or at the side of
Mary—but outside the stable, head in hands, bent, and
overwhelmed. What a mystery he was given to hide and
defend. First this woman, born without original sin—though
he knew nothing of this, only that she was different
somehow—and then this pregnancy. When we invite Mary
into our homes, we are inviting someone pure, powerful, and
potent, though we may not understand it fully.

Micah 5:1–4 or Romans 8:28–30
Psalm 13
Matthew 1:1–16, 18–23 or 1:18–23

SEPTEMBER 9

• ST. PETER CLAVER, PRIEST •

*Jesus departed to the mountain to pray, and he spent the night
in prayer to God. When day came, he called his disciples to
himself, and from them he chose Twelve, whom he also named
Apostles.*
—LUKE 6:12–13

A sleepless, full night of prayer precedes the naming of the
disciples.

Am I willing to make sacrifices to invest in the prayer
necessary before making the decisions that forge my life, my
future, and my heart?

1 Corinthians 6:1–11
Psalm 149
Luke 6:12–19

Wednesday

SEPTEMBER 10

"Blessed are you who are now weeping,
for you will laugh."
—LUKE 6:21

For what do you weep? Is it possible your tears are like holy
water, sanctifying your grief, blessing it, that one day it will
flourish and grow into joy?

1 Corinthians 7:25–31
Psalm 45
Luke 6:20–26

SEPTEMBER 11

*Knowledge inflates with pride, but love builds up. If anyone
supposes he knows something, he does not yet know as he
ought to know. But if one loves God, one is known by him.*
—1 CORINTHIANS 8:1–3

Thomas à Kempis writes, "God walks with sincere men,
reveals Himself to humble men, enlightens the
understanding of pure minds, and hides His grace from the
curious and the proud." There are so many warnings about
pride and conceit. Am I really listening? Do I see how
insidious it is, that pride is the proud papa of willfulness,
stubbornness, vanity, envy, every kind of deceit and
stupidity? It spends its life working against love and the true
knowledge of God.

Lord, hasten to remove my pride.

1 Corinthians 8:1b–7, 11–13
Psalm 139
Luke 6:27–38

Do you not know that the runners in the stadium all run in the race, but only one wins the prize? Run so as to win.
—1 CORINTHIANS 9:24

In an age when "everybody's a winner" and everyone gets a prize just for participating, we've lost a sense of the sacred fight, a holy sense of resistance and spiritual battle, because nothing is at stake. Or so the world would like us to believe. But in the race for holiness, where the prize is eternal life with God, everything is at stake. My triathlete brothers would say, "Leave it all on the course." In other words, run so as to win.

1 Corinthians 9:16–19, 22b–27
Psalm 84
Luke 6:39–42

SEPTEMBER 13

"For people do not pick figs from thornbushes, nor do they gather grapes from brambles. A good person out of the store of goodness in his heart produces good, but an evil person out of a store of evil produces evil; for from the fullness of the heart the mouth speaks."
—LUKE 6:44–45

Eventually our outsides catch up with our insides. A thorny heart can fake affection for only so long before it reveals its prickly nature. And you can't squeeze blood from a turnip. We cannot ask for good to flow from the heart of someone who does not have it within. But by loving the one whose heart is hardened, as John of the Cross says, you can put love where there was none.

1 Corinthians 10:14–22
Psalm 116
Luke 6:43–49

Sunday

SEPTEMBER 14

• THE EXALTATION OF THE HOLY CROSS •

Christ Jesus . . .
did not regard equality with God something to be grasped.
Rather, he emptied himself
. . . humbled himself,
becoming obedient to death,
even death on a cross.
—PHILIPPIANS 2:5–8

There is no clutching, but release; no striving, but surrender;
no filling up, only emptying; no assertion, but obedience.
And the end product of these paradoxes was not death, but
eternal life.

Numbers 21:4b–9
Psalm 78
Philippians 2:6–11
John 3:13–17

"Woman, behold, your son." Then he said to the disciple,
"Behold, your mother." And from that hour the disciple took her
into his home.
—JOHN 19:26–27

Even from the cross, Christ protects the family. What does
this say to me about my conduct with my own family? Do I
take great care with those entrusted to me?

1 Corinthians 11:17–26, 33
Psalm 40
John 19:25–27 or Luke 2:33–35

⇒ 289 ⇐

"Young man, I tell you, arise!" The dead man sat up and began to speak.
—LUKE 7:14–15

Every healing word that Jesus speaks is spoken to you, too. Every healing that takes place in the Gospel is your healing, too. Out of what dead place in your spirit is Jesus asking you to arise? Depression or abuse? Unconfessed sin, unforgiveness, resentment, or pride? Sickness, suffering, loneliness? He tells *you*, "Arise."

1 Corinthians 12:12–14, 27–31a
Psalm 100
Luke 7:11–17

Love is patient, love is kind. It is not jealous, love is not pompous, it is not inflated, it is not rude, it does not seek its own interests, it is not quick-tempered, it does not brood over injury, it does not rejoice over wrongdoing but rejoices with the truth. It bears all things, believes all things, hopes all things, endures all things. Love never fails.
—1 CORINTHIANS 13:4–8

St. Robert Bellarmine, noted for his intellectual prudence in the case of Galileo and the Counter-Reformation, and his great humility despite his position, is also remembered for his tenderness and devotion to the poor. He wrote, "The school of Christ is the school of charity. On the last day, when the general examination takes place, there will be no question at all on the text of Aristotle, the aphorisms of Hippocrates, or the paragraphs of Justinian. Charity will be the whole syllabus."

Lord, how are my studies coming for this test?

1 Corinthians 12:31—13:13
Psalm 33
Luke 7:31–35

"Your sins are forgiven."
—LUKE 7:48

She bathes the feet of Jesus with tears of repentance and thanksgiving, and he forgives her every sin. Every word of forgiveness spoken by Jesus in the Gospel is forgiveness offered to you, too. These words are spoken over you, ready for you and your tears of repentance, your tender kisses of thanksgiving, your great acts of love offered in recognition of all that Christ has already done for you.

1 Corinthians 15:1–11
Psalm 118
Luke 7:36–50

If Christ has not been raised, your faith is vain; you are still in your sins.
—1 CORINTHIANS 15:17

About two thousand years ago, a man tortured and crucified on a little hill in the middle of an ordinary afternoon, was buried for three days and mourned by not so many—until the appointed time when he raised himself from the dead. He left his burial place and walked the earth again, he spoke to friends and encouraged them, he ate and drank with them and appeared and disappeared in his mysterious resurrected body—the body that bore our sins so we wouldn't have to.

1 Corinthians 15:12–20
Psalm 17
Luke 8:1–3

SEPTEMBER 20

If there is a natural body, there is also a spiritual one.
—1 CORINTHIANS 15:44

Your body is—in every literal way you can understand the word—the temple of the Lord. This is why the Church is so interested in the dignity of the human person; your body is the home of your soul. You are hylomorphic; body and soul composite. And somehow, in some way we don't quite have the vocabulary for, your body will be resurrected at the appointed time, "raised glorious," "raised powerful," "raised."

1 Corinthians 15:35–37, 42–49
Psalm 56
Luke 8:4–15

SEPTEMBER 21

The LORD is gracious and merciful,
Slow to anger and of great kindness.
The LORD is good to all
And compassionate toward all his works.
—PSALM 145:8–9

A recovering addict once told me, "I know God's name and it is 'Mercy.'" Indeed. Mercy, Goodness, Great Kindness, the Compassionate One.

Lord, never let me forget your merciful hand, your gentle, tender heart.

Isaiah 55:6–9
Psalm 145
Philippians 1:20c–24, 27a
Matthew 20:1–16a

SEPTEMBER 22

*Refuse no one the good on which he has a claim
when it is in your power to do it for him.*
—PROVERBS 3:27

It is a serious sin to deliberately withhold the good from
someone—by withdrawing our love, affection, resources,
encouragement, engagement, or attention. When our spouse
or children, neighbors, friends, and strangers have a right to
our gifts and we fail to meet our obligations, we have sinned
by omission, and this sin is just as real as anything we might
"do" to others.

Proverbs 3:27–34
Psalm 15
Luke 8:16–18

SEPTEMBER 23

• ST. PIO OF PIETRELCINA, PRIEST •

All the ways of a man may be right in his own eyes,
but it is the LORD who proves hearts.
—PROVERBS 21:2

Does your heart belong entirely to Jesus? St. Pio wrote, "Prayer is the best weapon we have; it is the key to God's heart. You must speak to Jesus not only with your lips, but with your heart. In fact on certain occasions you should only speak to Him with your heart."

Jesus, know my heart.

Proverbs 21:1–6, 10–13
Psalm 119
Luke 8:19–21

Wednesday

SEPTEMBER 24

*From every evil way I withhold my feet,
that I may keep your words.*
—PSALM 119:101

We recoil from sin as though from a hot flame. Today, we
reject even the slightest temptation to sully ourselves. When
temptation comes, we choose the high road, we choose the
straight and loving path, we walk upright and humbly with
our God and trust that life abundant will keep us
company today.

Proverbs 30:5–9
Psalm 119
Luke 9:1–6

Thursday

SEPTEMBER 25

All things are vanity!
—ECCLESIASTES 1:2

Nothing proves vanity better than aging. Though I am not fond of this process, and I don't like the necessary losses incurred—like good sleep, energy, and a certain physical vitality—aging is a good gift in the ways it helps us grow in humility and the recognition of our dependence on God's grace for everything. My life, my relationships, my resources, and achievements have been given to me, and all will one day be returned.

Ecclesiastes 1:2–11
Psalm 90
Luke 9:7–9

Friday

SEPTEMBER 26

• ST. COSMAS AND ST. DAMIAN, MARTYRS •

A time to be silent, and a time to speak.
—ECCLESIASTES 3:7

Lord, be with me in my silence and in my speaking, that they
be informed by your wisdom, your love, and your truth. Give
me courage, poise, and when necessary an eloquent tongue.

Ecclesiastes 3:1–11
Psalm 144
Luke 9:18–22

Follow the ways of your heart,
the vision of your eyes;
Yet understand that as regards all this
God will bring you to judgment.
—ECCLESIASTES 11:9

We tend to be suspicious of our own desires, and with good reason. They can run riot with us, particularly if they are not ordered toward good ends. But the Lord is deeply invested in our heart's desires; he created us with them in mind. The life of the spirit is a continual discovery of which desires are God-given and which are not, and learning to fan the flame of all those that bring us into deeper communion with Jesus.

Ecclesiastes 11:9—12:8
Psalm 90
Luke 9:43b–45

*At the name of Jesus
every knee should bend,
of those in heaven and on earth and under the earth,
and every tongue confess that
Jesus Christ is Lord.*
—PHILIPPIANS 2:10–11

It is a common gesture among the seminarians I teach to bow their heads slightly at every mention of the name of Jesus during the Mass. In their quiet way, they honor that name above all names. To see their gentle devotion is a good reminder of what's at stake. The most powerful name ever to be uttered should be reverenced, and feared.

How do I hold and hail the name of Jesus?

Ezekiel 18:25–28
Psalm 25
Philippians 2:1–11 or 2:1–5
Matthew 21:28–32

SEPTEMBER 29

• ST. MICHAEL, ST. GABRIEL, AND ST. RAPHAEL, ARCHANGELS •

Thousands upon thousands were ministering to him,
and myriads upon myriads attended him.
—DANIEL 7:10

Though Daniel is describing a vision, we are invited to
ponder and possess all things "seen and unseen," the "visible
and invisible" blessings of God. Some of the great delight of
the Christian life is that so much of it is veiled from our
human senses; we need visions and dreams and visionaries to
help us enter the hidden wholeness of God's creation, where
angels come to visit, protect, and attend.

Daniel 7:9–10, 13–14 or
Revelation 12:7–12a
Psalm 138
John 1:47–51

I am a man without strength.
—PSALM 88:5

Yes, and I am a woman filled with weakness. How endlessly
and profoundly we need you, Lord! You meet us in our
frailties of mind and body, in our limp virtues and weakness
of heart. Jesus, today we collapse into your kind embrace,
and we trust your strength to protect us from all evil, and to
hold us up when we've reached our human limits.

Job 3:1–3, 11–17, 20–23
Psalm 88
Luke 9:51–56

Daily I call upon you, O LORD.
—PSALM 88:10

Is our daily discipline growing drab? The child says, "Mommy, do it again!" As G. K. Chesterton writes, "children have abounding vitality, because they are in spirit fierce and free, therefore they want things repeated and unchanged. . . . It is possible that God says every morning, 'Do it again' to the sun; and every evening 'Do it again' to the moon. It may not be automatic necessity that makes all daisies alike; it may be that God makes each daisy separately, but has never got tired of making them."

Job 9:1–12, 14–16
Psalm 88
Luke 9:57–62

Thursday

OCTOBER 2

• THE HOLY GUARDIAN ANGELS •

*"Their angels in heaven always look upon the face of my
heavenly Father."*
—MATTHEW 18:10

Why should the angels of children hold so exalted a place?
In a culture that tends to view children as commodities,
liabilities, or products, we might lose sight of the riches of
childlike humility and innocence. We might cease to
recognize the certain value of all life and the economy of
heaven wherein humility and innocence are lauded above all.

Job 19:21–27
Psalm 27
Matthew 18:1–5, 10

OCTOBER 3

*Have you ever in your lifetime commanded the morning
and shown the dawn its place . . . ?*

*. . . Have you entered into the sources of the sea,
or walked about in the depths of the abyss?
Have the gates of death been shown to you,
or have you seen the gates of darkness?
Have you comprehended the breadth of the earth?*
—JOB 38:12, 16–18

Job—a righteous man—is taking it on the chin. He clearly
understands that being in right relationship with the creator
of heaven and earth is the surest and fastest way out of his
own misery.

Lord, let every ounce of suffering I encounter—little or
great—teach me something about your majesty, your power,
and your purpose.

Job 38:1, 12–21; 40:3–5
Psalm 139
Luke 10:13–16

Saturday

OCTOBER 4

• ST. FRANCIS OF ASSISI, RELIGIOUS •

Job answered the LORD and said,
"I know that you can do all things,
and that no purpose of yours can be hindered.
I have dealt with great things that I do not understand;
things too wonderful for me, which I cannot know. . . .
Therefore I disown what I have said,
and repent in dust and ashes."

Thus the LORD blessed the latter days of Job more than his
earlier ones . . . Job died, old and full of years.
—JOB 42:1–3, 6, 12, 17

Crime does not pay, but repentance surely does. The Lord does bless; he makes our days and years full and rich and too wonderful. His justice always brings about our flourishing.

Job 42:1–3, 5–6, 12–17
Psalm 119
Luke 10:17–24

⋛ 308 ⋚

OCTOBER 5

Give us new life, and we will call upon your name.
O LORD, God of hosts, restore us;
if your face shine upon us, then we shall be saved.
—PSALM 80:19–20

God never forces himself on us; rather we cooperate with grace and restoration. As much as we might hope that God will do all the work for us, we do have to participate in his plan of salvation with, at the very least, an inward turning, an acknowledgement of his name and the power to be invoked there. And even then, we must be willing to receive new life. These are often painful propositions, but God will be with us in this work.

Isaiah 5:1–7
Psalm 80
Philippians 4:6–9
Matthew 21:33–43

OCTOBER 6

• BLESSED MARIE-ROSE DUROCHER, VIRGIN •

"The Gospel preached by me is not of human origin. For I did not receive it from a human being, nor was I taught it, but it came through a revelation of Jesus Christ."
—GALATIANS 1:11–12

Some things we know by birth into the natural world, and some things we know by baptism into the supernatural order. Some things we know by reason, and some things we know by revelation. Our faith asks us to hold in a dynamic tension reason and faith—natural and supernatural realities. We learn to trust that those things we know by revelation—even though they may be difficult to embrace and understand—are revealed by love, in love, and through the love of Christ.

Galatians 1:6–12
Psalm 111
Luke 10:25–37

With all my ways you are familiar.
—PSALM 139:3

It is a great good that God knows me in all my ways,
especially those ways that are sinful and self-destructive. It is
a comfort to be completely vulnerable with God in
confession and reconciliation, knowing that he knows me
perfectly. Pretense of any kind is simply useless.

Galatians 1:13–24
Psalm 139
Luke 10:38–42

*"And when Cephas came to Antioch, I opposed him to his face
because he clearly was wrong."*
—GALATIANS 2:11

I would do virtually anything to avoid conflict. But that
simply is not the reality of Christian life: we must protect
those who cannot protect themselves; we must speak for
those who cannot speak for themselves; we must stand up for
the truth when it is under attack. We must confront—in
love, wisdom, and prudence—those who wrong us. We
cannot really call ourselves Christians unless we are, in the
ways we are called, fighting the good fight.

Galatians 2:1–2, 7–14
Psalm 117
Luke 11:1–4

Thursday

OCTOBER 9

Jesus said to his disciples: "Suppose one of you has a friend to whom he goes at midnight and says, 'Friend, lend me three loaves of bread, for a friend of mine has arrived at my house from a journey and I have nothing to offer him.'"
—LUKE 11:5–6

One thing we often overlook about this passage is that the friend is asking for bread—not for himself, but for another. His request is a kind of intercession. Jesus' promise, "Ask and you will receive," of course applies to our needs, but in this case, the friend's persistence was on behalf of another. It tells us how very powerful our persistent prayers for others really are.

Galatians 3:1–5
Luke 1:69–70, 71–72, 73–75
Luke 11:5–13

"When an unclean spirit goes out of someone, it roams through arid regions searching for rest but, finding none, it says, 'I shall return to my home from which I came.' But upon returning, it finds it swept clean and put in order. Then it goes and brings back seven other spirits more wicked than itself who move in and dwell there, and the last condition of that man is worse than the first."
—LUKE 11:24–26

"Is it dangerous to be delivered by Jesus from an evil spirit?" asks theologian Hans Urs von Balthasar. "Perhaps not dangerous, but it certainly brings some responsibilities. . . . The house may well be 'spruced up' yet still be empty, since it remains for the cleansed person to fill it with new life. Jesus' words . . . apply equally well to anyone who has received absolution for his sins—here too something has been removed from the person, something that had become part of himself as he consented to sin."

Galatians 3:7–14
Psalm 111
Luke 11:15–26

*For all of you who were baptized into Christ have clothed
yourselves with Christ. There is neither Jew nor Greek, there is
neither slave nor free person, there is not male and female; for
you are all one in Christ Jesus.*
—GALATIANS 3:27–28

Is Paul suggesting that we are all one big homogenous blob?
That the Christian life necessarily entails the loss of our
"individuality," those things that make us unique and
unrepeatable? It is a great paradox that we are one in Christ
and free, unique creations at the same time. As the Trinity is
three in one, so the Church body is multiple and singular.
The important question is, what keeps me from communion
with my brethren, and with God?

Galatians 3:22–29
Psalm 105
Luke 11:27–28

*On this mountain he will destroy
the veil that veils all peoples,
the web that is woven over all nations;
he will destroy death forever.*
—ISAIAH 25:7–8

One day, maybe sooner than you think, you will be given
the opportunity to step into the true light of reality, where
the invisible will be made visible, where eternity will enfold
you and draw you into perfect communion with the Creator
of All. And all that hangs from your shoulders now—the
burdens, the unanswered questions, the fears and terrors of
so many dark nights—will be lifted forever, never to return.

Isaiah 25:6–10a
Psalm 23
Philippians 4:12–14, 19–20
Matthew 22:1–14 or 22:1–10

*For freedom, Christ set us free; so stand firm and do not submit
again to the yoke of slavery.*
—GALATIANS 5:1

Jesus was clear to say that it's the truth that makes us free.
"Conversion," writes A. D. Serillanges, "means a willingness
to see the truth of things and conform one's conduct to it."
Conversion, truth, and the freedom to love are bound up in
one another; we cannot have one without the other two.

Galatians 4:22–24, 26–27, 31—5:1
Psalm 113
Luke 11:29–32

Let your mercy come to me, O LORD,
your salvation according to your promise.
—PSALM 119:41

Mercy comes when I'm willing to live in reality, to accept the truth about myself. Acceptance is in fact the first harbinger of mercy's arrival. Sometimes I need help from others close to me to see myself as I really am. Am I willing to allow trusted friends to correct my own ideas about myself? Am I willing to be guided and challenged and sometimes confronted about the areas in which I need to grow? Will I allow mercy to visit me this way?

Galatians 5:1–6
Psalm 119
Luke 11:37–41

⇒ 318 ⇐

OCTOBER 15

• ST. TERESA OF ÁVILA, VIRGIN AND DOCTOR OF THE CHURCH •

Now those who belong to Christ Jesus have crucified their flesh
with its passions and desires.
—GALATIANS 5:24

Mortification has rather fallen out of fashion. Much
psychology would put Teresa of Ávila and other saints on
medication for her mortifications and general disposition.
We remember, though, the precariousness of life without
penicillin, clean water, and housing, some of the things we
now take for granted. Teresa's point is this: "Our body has
this defect that, the more it is provided care and comforts,
the more needs and desires it finds." A little self-denial could
go a long way in freeing us to love well.

Galatians 5:18–25
Psalm 1
Luke 11:42–46

Thursday

OCTOBER 16

• ST. HEDWIG, RELIGIOUS; ST. MARGARET MARY ALACOQUE, VIRGIN •

*He chose us . . . before the foundation of the world, to be holy
and without blemish before him.*
—EPHESIANS 1:4

We have been chosen before all creation, but to be a chosen
people is to be shown favor—in holiness and virtue. We are
not exempted from the trials that produce holiness and
virtue; rather we are blessed with them, selected for them,
and graced for them.

When next suffering befalls me, Lord, remind me that you
chose me before the foundation of the world.

Ephesians 1:1–10
Psalm 98
Luke 11:47–54

From heaven the LORD looks down;
he sees all mankind.
—PSALM 33:13

St. Vincent Ferrer is attributed with saying, "Whatever you do, think not of yourself, but of God."

Indeed, God thinks of nothing but you.

Ephesians 1:11–14
Psalm 33
Luke 12:1–7

Saturday

OCTOBER 18

• ST. LUKE, EVANGELIST •

The Lord Jesus appointed seventy-two disciples whom he sent
ahead of him in pairs.
—LUKE 10:1

Though there may be occasions where the Lord asks me to
stand alone, more often than not, he'll send me a companion.
Community not only protects me from external dangers and
attacks, but close companions protect me from internal
dangers, such as pride, envy, dishonesty, and every kind of
sin that might fool me into thinking I can do it alone. We are
a communal people, even in the way we are to evangelize the
culture. We do it together.

2 Timothy 4:10–17b
Psalm 145
Luke 10:1–9

For our gospel did not come to you in word alone, but also in power and in the Holy Spirit and with much conviction.
—1 THESSALONIANS 1:5

Our encounter with the divine is not merely an experience of reading words on a page and then sitting still, thinking great thoughts about them—though this is certainly an important part of the life of the Spirit. But it does not end on a page or in a thought; it moves forward toward heaven in the power of actions fed by hearts deeply in love with the Truth.

Isaiah 45:1, 4–6
Psalm 96
1 Thessalonians 1:1–5b
Matthew 22:15–21

For we are his handiwork, created in Christ Jesus for good works that God has prepared in advance, that we should live in them.
—EPHESIANS 2:10

You are a moral agent, and you were created for good—to live in goodness, good works, good friendships, good families and communities. Sin rips us away from the very intention behind our creation. Living outside the intention for which we are created brings some of the greatest pain there is. In this sense, Jesus is asking you to be exactly who you were created to be—goodness walking around in the world.

Ephesians 2:1–10
Psalm 100
Luke 12:13–21

Blessed are those servants whom the master finds vigilant on his
arrival.
—LUKE 12:37

What would it take to make you ready? Reconciliation, more
prayer, a good long retreat? A better sense of your resources
as available to the Church, more time spent in service to
others? Forgiveness—of yourself or someone else? More rest
on the Sabbath, more study, less television? More fasting,
less indulgence? What would it take to be found ready and
vigilant?

Ephesians 2:12–22
Psalm 85
Luke 12:35–38

God indeed is my savior;
I am confident and unafraid.
My strength and my courage is the LORD,
and he has been my savior.
—ISAIAH 12:2

Strength and courage aren't always obvious. Blessed Mother Teresa said, "We are at Jesus' disposal. If he wants you to be sick in bed, if he wants you to proclaim His work in the street, if he wants you to clean the toilets all day, that's all right, everything is all right. We must say, 'I belong to you. You can do whatever you like.' And this," she says, "is our strength, and this is the joy of the Lord."

Ephesians 3:2–12
Isaiah 12:2–3, 4bcd, 5–6
Luke 12:39–48

Thursday

OCTOBER 23

"I have come to set the earth on fire, and how I wish it were already blazing!"
—LUKE 12:49

Fire doesn't so much destroy something as change the form of the thing it consumes. Ashes make excellent fertilizer. Our hearts must be consumed—set ablaze by Christ—not so they can be destroyed, but so that they can be transformed into a fecund place for true love to grow and flourish.

Ephesians 3:14–21
Psalm 33
Luke 12:49–53

*I, a prisoner for the Lord, urge you to live . . . with all humility
and gentleness, with patience, bearing with one another
through love, striving to preserve the unity of the spirit through
the bond of peace.*
—EPHESIANS 4:1–3

Bearing with one another is much tougher than it sounds. But
sometimes, all it takes is one stilling breath, one more beat of
thought to say, all right, let's go a little easy on one another.
Humility, gentleness, patience—these are welcomed by the
tenderhearted, the one who takes the time to cultivate a deep
appreciation for the bonds of peace.

Jesus, give me a tender, gentle heart, so that just for today, I
may be an agent of peace.

Ephesians 4:1–6
Psalm 24
Luke 12:54–59

OCTOBER 25

So that we may no longer be infants, tossed by waves and swept along by every wind of teaching arising from human trickery. . . . Rather, living the truth in love, we should grow in every way into him who is the head, Christ, from whom the whole Body, joined and held together by every supporting ligament, with the proper functioning of each part, brings about the Body's growth and builds itself up in love.
—EPHESIANS 4:14–16

Growing the Church body, so diverse in all her gifts, is a work of great patience and perseverance. It requires wisdom beyond the sum of its parts, grace from another world, and a certain sacred imagination. Like a child in the womb, unaware of the broader world around it, we rely on the prayers of saints and angels and heaven's provision and remain very much a part of the whole Body of Christ—visible and invisible. Part of our proper functioning, whatever our gifts, is to recognize this.

Ephesians 4:7–16
Psalm 122
Luke 13:1–9

Sunday

OCTOBER 26

*"You shall love the Lord, your God, with all your heart, with all
your soul, and with all your mind. . . . You shall love your
neighbor as yourself. The whole law and the prophets depend
on these two commandments."*
—MATTHEW 22:37–40

A great dynamic tension rises up over the life of the
Christian. Though the nature of these commandments may
be slightly different, we take note that each law is in fact
grounded in love. The extraordinary thing is that they
complement each other perfectly; like light and darkness, or
walls and roof—they do not exist outside each other but
together create the whole.

What sheer delight, O Lord, to ponder your commands.

Exodus 22:20–26
Psalm 18
1 Thessalonians 1:5c–10
Matthew 22:34–40

OCTOBER 27

Live as children of light.
—EPHESIANS 5:8

"Children of light" is further defined: no obscenity or silly or suggestive talk; immorality or impurity or greed "must not even be mentioned among you." Quite a standard. One would have to wear blinders to move through the checkout line and not see the gossip magazines. But is that really so much to ask? To avert the eye, to turn away from the darkness and immorality sprawling across our world's billboards, advertisements, and televisions? Isn't "chastity of the eyes" central to living as a child of light?

Ephesians 4:32—5:8
Psalm 1
Luke 13:10–17

*Through him the whole structure is held together and grows
into a temple sacred in the Lord; in him you also are being built
together into a dwelling place of God in the Spirit.*
—EPHESIANS 2:21–22

You are part of the larger narrative of salvation history; larger
than the history of humanity. The sacred dwelling is *you*, the
temple is *you*—your body, your spirit, and your gifts. Your
being is the structure God himself holds together—for the
sake of holiness and eternal purpose.

Ephesians 2:19–22
Psalm 19
Luke 6:12–16

OCTOBER 29

Children obey your parents in the Lord, for this is right. "Honor
your father and mother." This is the first commandment with a
promise, "that it may go well with you and that you may have a
long life on earth."
—EPHESIANS 6:1–3

Lauri's mother was mentally ill; her father, an alcoholic,
abandoned the family when Lauri was young. For her safety
and the safety of her children, she learned to honor her
father and mother—from a distance—in her heart, in her
prayers, in the ways she parented her own children. And her
life became living reparation for the sins of others.

Ephesians 6:1–9
Psalm 145
Luke 13:22–30

*Pray at every opportunity in the Spirit . . . that I may have the
courage to speak as I must.*
—EPHESIANS 6:18, 20

In this dark time, when little girls are aborted before they are
born in China, and boys and girls are aborted in the United
States by the millions each year, when the organs of healthy
prisoners are auctioned off to the highest bidder in foreign
lands, when disease from our polluted water and soil and sky
rises every day, and where meanness is sold at the box office
and turned into a virtue—Lord, give us the courage to speak
as we must.

Ephesians 6:10–20
Psalm 144
Luke 13:31–35

*"Who among you, if your son or ox falls into a cistern, would
not immediately pull him out on the sabbath day?"*
—LUKE 14:5

The love of Christ removes the boundaries and obstacles
that keep us from his embrace. And his embrace is precisely
this, from the cross, stretching in every direction into
eternity. There is no one, no pain, no sin, hidden from his
loving arms.

Philippians 1:1–11
Psalm 111
Luke 14:1–6

Saturday

NOVEMBER 1

• ALL SAINTS •

*"Salvation comes from our God, who is seated on the throne,
and from the Lamb. . . .
Blessing and glory, wisdom and thanksgiving,
honor, power, and might
be to our God forever and ever. Amen."*
—REVELATION 7:10, 12

Saints become saints in part because they begin the work of
heaven in their earthly lives. And the work of heaven is
always praise and honor and glory, the perfect worship of
the Lamb.

Revelation 7:2–4, 9–14
Psalm 24
1 John 3:1–3
Matthew 5:1–12a

NOVEMBER 2

Sunday

• COMMEMORATION OF ALL THE FAITHFUL DEPARTED (ALL SOULS) •

For this is the will of my Father, that everyone who sees the Son and believes in him may have eternal life, and I shall raise him up on the last day.
—JOHN 6:40

If you believed that Jesus is the resurrection, how would your day change?

Wisdom 3:1–9
Psalm 23
Romans 5:5–11 or Romans 6:3–9
John 6:37–40
Other readings may be selected.

NOVEMBER 3

• ST. MARTIN DE PORRES, RELIGIOUS •

O LORD, my heart is not proud,
nor are my eyes haughty;
I busy not myself with great things,
nor with things too sublime for me.
Nay, rather, I have stilled and quieted
my soul like a weaned child.
Like a weaned child on its mother's lap,
so is my soul within me.
—PSALM 131:1–2

Today, Jesus, I will live little and low. I will do my duty in love and gratitude; I will live my vocation and love those around me in simplicity of heart. I will stay low that others may be raised; I will listen as others speak. My soul will rest in the acceptance of a quiet, anonymous day.

Philippians 2:1–4
Psalm 131
Luke 14:12–14

Tuesday

NOVEMBER 4

• ST. CHARLES BORROMEO, BISHOP •

He emptied himself . . .
he humbled himself,
becoming obedient to death.
—PHILIPPIANS 2:7–8

When my ire is raised, when I want to resist your grace,
when I want to push against your guidance and every virtue,
when I want to fill myself with pride and earthly
satisfactions, Jesus, I make my oath your oath: empty me,
humble me, help me obey.

Philippians 2:5–11
Psalm 22
Luke 14:15–24

⋙ 339 ⋘

NOVEMBER 5

In the midst of a crooked and perverse generation, among whom you shine like lights in the world . . .
—PHILIPPIANS 2:15

The truth doesn't need a marketing campaign; it simply needs to *be*, keeping company with her sisters, goodness and beauty. "We do not draw other people to Christ," writes Madeleine L'Engle, "by loudly discrediting what they believe, by telling them how wrong they are and how right we are, but by showing them a light that is so lovely that they want with all their hearts to know the source of it."

Philippians 2:12–18
Psalm 27
Luke 14:25–33

NOVEMBER 6

"There will be rejoicing among the angels of God over one sinner who repents."
—LUKE 15:10

Want to make an angel happy? Go make a thorough confession.

Philippians 3:3–8a
Psalm 105
Luke 15:1–10

He will change our lowly body to conform with his glorified Body by the power that enables him also to bring all things into subjection to himself.
—PHILIPPIANS 3:21

The body is critically important, but not for the reasons that the body-insecurity business suggests. As hylomorphic creatures—composites of soul and flesh—our bodies take on a significance that Madison Avenue cannot touch. Your body has been created out of an eternal being with an eternal purpose. It houses your eternal soul and thus is a reflection of it.

Lord, help me treat my body with proper dignity—in fasting and mortification, in modesty and moderation.

Philippians 3:17—4:1
Psalm 122
Luke 16:1–8

NOVEMBER 8

*I know indeed how to live in humble circumstances; I know also
how to live with abundance. In every circumstance and in all
things I have learned the secret of being well fed and of going
hungry, of living in abundance and of being in need. I have the
strength for everything through him who empowers me.*
—PHILIPPIANS 4:12–13

Most of us live in the middle—neither in lavishness nor in
poverty. Empowerment comes to Paul not in his
circumstances, but in God. Joseph Cardinal Ratzinger wrote
that "Being a Christian does not mean some special skill
alongside other skills but simply the correct living out of
being human, we could also say that we want to practice the
skill of living correctly: we want to learn better the skill of
skills, the art of being human." Indeed, "in every
circumstance and in all things."

Philippians 4:10–19
Psalm 112
Luke 16:9–15

———————

⟩ 343 ⟨

You are God's building.
—1 CORINTHIANS 3:9

Blessed John Paul II reminds us in *Evangelium Vitae*, "Man's life comes from God; it is his gift, his image and imprint, a sharing in his breath of life. God therefore is the sole Lord of this life: man cannot do with it as he wills . . . The sacredness of life gives rise to its inviolability, written from the beginning in man's heart, in his conscience . . . in the depths of his conscience, man is always reminded of the inviolability of life—his own life and that of others—as something which does not belong to him, because it is the property and gift of God the Creator and Father."

Ezekiel 47:1–2, 8–9, 12
Psalm 46
1 Corinthians 3:9c–11, 16–17
John 2:13–22

NOVEMBER 10

• ST. LEO THE GREAT, POPE AND DOCTOR OF THE CHURCH •

For a bishop as God's steward must be blameless . . . a lover of goodness, temperate, just, holy, and self-controlled, holding fast to the true message as taught so that he will be able both to exhort with sound doctrine and to refute opponents.
—TITUS 1:7–9

All of Christian life is a challenge to grow in virtue, but leadership in the Church is particularly demanding. Today, let us pray for our priests, religious, deacons, bishops, cardinals, and the Holy Father—that God may endow them with every gift required to lead us in exhortation and refutation of those who would oppose Church teaching.

Titus 1:1–9
Psalm 24
Luke 17:1–6

Turn from evil and do good.
—PSALM 37:27

Do you tend to complicate things? Overanalyze or obfuscate situations? Assign sophisticated nuance where perhaps none is needed? The psalmist is clear, gentle, and direct. This trio of qualities can often serve us when we are making decisions.

Titus 2:1–8, 11–14
Psalm 37
Luke 17:7–10

NOVEMBER 12

• ST. JOSAPHAT, BISHOP AND MARTYR •

We ourselves were once foolish, disobedient, deluded, slaves to
various desires and pleasures, living in malice and envy, hateful
ourselves and hating one another.
But when the kindness and generous love
of God our savior appeared . . .
because of his mercy,
he saved us.
—TITUS 3:3–5

We imagine the foolish, the disobedient and debauched, the
envious and resentful, and we do not want to think of
ourselves in that ugly picture. You know your struggle. You
know how these verses might be applied to you. You know,
too, that the love of God is kind and generous and merciful
enough to save you if you really want to change.

Titus 3:1–7
Psalm 23
Luke 17:11–19

Thursday

NOVEMBER 13

• ST. FRANCES XAVIER CABRINI, VIRGIN •

The LORD sets captives free.
—PSALM 146:7

Freedom can be eradicated by many things: fear, addiction,
greed, pride, hardness of heart, resentment, laziness, fear of
doing the right thing, fear of saying something difficult that
needs to be said. Today, I place the thing that binds me in
your hands, O Lord. I believe in your plan for my freedom to
choose the good. Today, I ask for the grace to cooperate
with all that is true, good, and beautiful.

Philemon 1:7–20
Psalm 146
Luke 17:20–25

NOVEMBER 14

Remember the wife of Lot.
—LUKE 17:32

The temptation to turn our eyes toward evil is great,
even—or perhaps especially—for those sincere souls
engaged in the life of the Spirit. It can deceive us with a false
allure. Am I watchful, Lord? What do I let in? What do I
allow to cross the threshold—through what I read, watch,
listen to, think about, or in the company I keep?

2 John 1:4–9
Psalm 119
Luke 17:26–37

*Jesus told his disciples a parable about the necessity for them to
pray always without becoming weary.*
—LUKE 18:1

If we didn't grow weary at times, we wouldn't need this
parable. But Jesus knows that we do. Essentially we are given
heaven's permission to be a bother. When weariness
threatens, go "bother" heaven awhile. It's not only allowed,
but encouraged.

3 John 1:5–8
Psalm 112
Luke 18:1–8

Sunday

NOVEMBER 16

When one finds a worthy wife,
her value is far beyond pearls.
Her husband, entrusting his heart to her,
has an unfailing prize.
She brings him good, and not evil,
all the days of her life.
—PROVERBS 31:10–12

These verses could be said of husbands as well. To find
someone to whom we can truly entrust our hearts is a gift
indeed. Today we pray for the strength of marriages, for
those preparing for marriage, those married a long while, and
those who struggle in painful marriages. Lord, teach us how
to truly entrust ourselves to another. Make us worthy that
our loved ones may entrust their hearts to us.

Proverbs 31:10–13, 19–20, 30–31
Psalm 128
1 Thessalonians 5:1–6
Matthew 25:14–30 or 25:14–15, 19–21

⇒ 351 ⇐

NOVEMBER 17

• ST. ELIZABETH OF HUNGARY, RELIGIOUS •

*You have lost the love you had at first. Realize how far you have
fallen. Repent, and do the works you did at first.*
—REVELATION 2:4–5

In every love relationship, there are times when we need
reminding of why we fell in love in the first place.

Lord, ignite my fervency. Give me a heart that is renewed in
its delight over your perfect love, forgiveness, and generous
blessing.

Revelation 1:1–4; 2:1–5
Psalm 1
Luke 18:35–43

⇒ 352 ⇐

Tuesday

NOVEMBER 18

• ST. ROSE PHILIPPINE DUCHESNE, VIRGIN •

Those whom I love, I reprove and chastise.
—REVELATION 3:19

I once jumped into the water of a lake directly behind the whirring blade of a motor boat. I did not see the danger beneath the water; but my father did. He yelled at me to move away. He was furious—for my safety. A vision of my young limbs being chopped to shreds filled his heart. His scolding scared me at first, but I never jumped into the water again behind a motor boat with the engine running, and all my limbs remain intact.

Revelation 3:1–6, 14–22
Psalm 15
Luke 19:1–10

*"Worthy are you, Lord our God,
to receive glory and honor and power,
for you created all things;
because of your will they came to be and were created."*
—REVELATION 4:11

Science leans more and more in the direction of creation as the act of a supra-intellect. Fr. Robert Spitzer, working in cosmology—the study of the origins of the universe—notes that if God were to stop thinking of us, we'd cease to exist. "If God stops thinking us into existence, we would become nothing. God is an absolutely simple, unique, continuous Creator of all else that is."

Revelation 4:1–11
Psalm 150
Luke 19:11–28

As Jesus drew near Jerusalem, he saw the city and wept over it,
saying, "If this day you only knew what makes for peace."
—LUKE 19:41–42

It is difficult to imagine Jesus upset; so rarely is he depicted
so in the Gospels. All the more reason we note that his
lament for us lies in our ignorance, our inability to live
peaceably. Some things never change.

Revelation 5:1–10
Psalm 149
Luke 19:41–44

Your decrees are my inheritance forever;
the joy of my heart they are.
I gasp with open mouth
in my yearning for your commands.
—PSALM 119:111, 131

Spend some time today meditating on one of God's "laws"
that simply takes your breath away: the beginning of
life—ensoulment—at conception; the creation of the
cosmos—stars and planets and space; the mystery of
sacramental reality, water into wine; the healing of the
woman with the hemorrhage; the forgiveness of sins; the
Word made flesh, who dwelt among us.

Revelation 10:8–11
Psalm 119
Luke 19:45–48

"He is not God of the dead, but of the living, for to him all are alive."
—LUKE 20:38

"Only eternity sees time as a whole," writes Peter Kreeft. "Time is life spilled out, like a bucket of water spilled on the ground. Eternity is the togetherness of all the water in the bucket. It is time come home. Boethius gave the classic definition of eternity as 'the whole, perfect and simultaneous possession of endless life.' From this God's-eye point of view 'all things work together for good.' . . . Nothing is missing; nothing is lost; nothing goes down the drain."

Revelation 11:4–12
Psalm 144
Luke 20:27–40

Sunday

NOVEMBER 23

• OUR LORD JESUS CHRIST THE KING •

*"For I was hungry and you gave me food, I was thirsty and you
gave me drink, a stranger and you welcomed me, naked and you
clothed me, ill and you cared for me, in prison and you
visited me."*
—MATTHEW 25:35–36

We know these acts as the corporal works of mercy, and they
are offered to us not like a laundry list of virtuous tasks, but
as a way of life. They allow us to see Jesus in everyone,
everywhere, in every circumstance.

Ezekiel 34:11–12, 15–17
Psalm 23
1 Corinthians 15:20–26, 28
Matthew 25:31–46

NOVEMBER 24

• ST. ANDREW DUNG-LAC, PRIEST AND MARTYR, AND COMPANIONS, MARTYRS •

On their lips no deceit has been found; they are unblemished.
—REVELATION 14:5

The 144,000 are marked by honesty and purity. St. Vincent de Paul reminds us that "Humility is nothing but truth, and pride is nothing but lying." This is why the truth sets us free from the bondage to self. And why we continually ask God for the grace to keep from deceiving ourselves about our own fallenness.

Revelation 14:1–3, 4b–5
Psalm 24
Luke 21:1–4

Tuesday

NOVEMBER 25

"See that you not be deceived."
—LUKE 21:8

Do I toy with the truth? Stretch things? Occasionally let myself off the hook with the little white lie, the meager self-deception? Today I will do a thorough examination of conscience, looking especially for sins against the truth: rash judgment, calumny, detraction, flattery, boasting, and the lies that lead to greater sins such as pornography and social injustice.

Revelation 14:14–19
Psalm 96
Luke 21:5–11

NOVEMBER 26

You alone are holy.
—REVELATION 15:4

You alone are the Most High, Jesus Christ, with the Holy
Spirit, in the glory of God the Father. Amen.

Holy, holy, holy Lord.

Revelation 15:1–4
Psalm 98
Luke 21:12–19

⩾ 361 ⩽

Blessed are those who have been called to the wedding feast of the Lamb.
—REVELATION 19:9

The Lamb's wedding feast is the most important feast in all the world—and you're invited. There is a place reserved just for you.

Revelation 18:1–2, 21–23; 19:1–3, 9a
Psalm 100
Luke 21:20–28

NOVEMBER 28

"Heaven and earth will pass away, but my words will not pass away."
—LUKE 21:33

Where do I anchor myself? How do I move through this passing world? How does a sacramental reality open me to the world that does not pass away?

Revelation 20:1–4, 11—21:2
Psalm 84
Luke 21:29–33

NOVEMBER 29

In his hands are the depths of the earth,
and the tops of the mountains are his.
His is the sea, for he has made it,
and the dry land, which his hands have formed.
Come, let us bow down in worship;
let us kneel before the LORD who made us.
—PSALM 95:4–6

We can correct any identity crisis by considering the God who made us. All of nature reminds us of his majesty, power, and creativity. As pope emeritus Benedict XVI has said, "We are not some casual and meaningless product of evolution. Each of us is the result of a thought of God. Each of us is willed, each of us is loved, each of us is necessary."

Revelation 22:1–7
Psalm 95
Luke 21:34–36

Why do you let us wander, O LORD, from your ways,
and harden our hearts so that we fear you not?
Return for the sake of your servants.
—ISAIAH 63:17

The cry of Advent is the great cry of the human spirit:
Come, Lord Jesus. Even those trapped in hardness of heart
long to be released from it.

Today we pray for deeper conversion.

Isaiah 63:16b–17, 19b; 64:2–7
Psalm 80
1 Corinthians 1:3–9
Mark 13:33–37

DECEMBER 1

"Lord, I am not worthy to have you enter under my roof."
—MATTHEW 8:8

All of Advent is about precisely this: welcoming Jesus into
our homes and lives, welcoming him as King, Savior, Friend,
and Father. Our worthiness has nothing to do with it. Our
willingness—or willfulness—has everything to do with it.

Isaiah 2:1–5
Psalm 122
Matthew 8:5–11

The Spirit of the LORD shall rest upon him:
a Spirit of wisdom and of understanding,
A Spirit of counsel and of strength,
a Spirit of knowledge and of fear of the LORD.
—ISAIAH 11:2

We recognize God's Spirit by the character and fruit of the
Spirit: wisdom, understanding, counsel, strength, knowledge,
holy fear, or right relationship with God.

Isaiah 11:1–10
Psalm 72
Luke 10:21–24

Wednesday
DECEMBER 3

• ST. FRANCIS XAVIER, PRIEST •

The LORD God will wipe away
the tears from all faces.
—ISAIAH 25:8

It was just one of those years, a stretch of life marked by every kind of suffering. It was not one thing in particular but everything all at once. We get knocked down sometimes, our hope erodes suddenly under the weight of our fallen nature.

But this is why the communal nature of the Church is so incredibly potent and real; if your hope has run out, you can borrow some of mine. One day, you will return the favor.

Isaiah 25:6–10a
Psalm 23
Matthew 15:29–37

DECEMBER 4

• ST. JOHN DAMASCENE, PRIEST AND DOCTOR OF THE CHURCH •

Give thanks to the LORD, for he is good.
—PSALM 118:1

There is very little wrong in the world, very few errant moods of the heart, that a good dose of rightly ordered gratitude will not cure. Cultivating a grateful heart is a habit that builds upon itself. When we are mindful of this disposition, it becomes easier and easier to find the good—the goodness of God—in all things, all people, all circumstances.

Isaiah 26:1–6
Psalm 118
Matthew 7:21, 24–27

DECEMBER 5

Wait for the LORD with courage.
—PSALM 27:14

That's courage, little one, not wringing hands, not impatience, not foreboding. Courage.

St. George, patron saint of bravery, pray for us.

Isaiah 29:17–24
Psalm 27
Matthew 9:27–31

⇒ 370 ⇐

*At the sight of the crowds, his heart was moved with pity for
them because they were troubled and abandoned, like sheep
without a shepherd.*
—MATTHEW 9:36

Pope emeritus Benedict XVI said it this way: "I think we
should meditate upon this reality. Christ stands before God
and is praying for me. His prayer on the Cross is
contemporary with all human beings, contemporary with
me. He prays for me, he suffered and suffers for me, he
identified himself with me, taking our body and the human
soul. And he asks us to enter this identity of his, making
ourselves one body, one spirit with him."

Isaiah 30:19–21, 23–26
Psalm 147
Matthew 9:35—10:1, 5a, 6–8

Comfort, give comfort to my people,
says your God.
Speak tenderly to Jerusalem.
—ISAIAH 40:1–2

Tenderness is a basic human need. Karol Wojtyla writes in
Love and Responsibility that "[t]enderness is the ability to
feel with and for the whole person, to feel even the most
deeply hidden spiritual tremors, and always to have in mind
the true good of that person. . . . [T]enderness creates a
feeling of not being alone, a feeling that [one's] whole life is
equally the content of another and very dear person's life.
This conviction very greatly facilitates and reinforces their
sense of unity."

Isaiah 40:1–5, 9–11
Psalm 85
2 Peter 3:8–14
Mark 1:1–8

DECEMBER 8

• IMMACULATE CONCEPTION OF THE BLESSED VIRGIN MARY •

*He chose us in him, before the foundation of the world, to be
holy and without blemish before him.*
—EPHESIANS 1:4

Because of her purity and her unique place in the order of
things, the Blessed Mother can be an especially powerful
intercessor on behalf of those who struggle with sexual sins
that fill us with darkness and shame.

Immaculate Heart of Mary, pray for us.

Genesis 3:9–15, 20
Psalm 98
Ephesians 1:3–6, 11–12
Luke 1:26–38

*If a man has a hundred sheep and one of them goes astray, will
he not leave the ninety-nine in the hills and go in search of the
stray? And if he finds it, amen, I say to you, he rejoices more
over it than over the ninety-nine that did not stray.*
—MATTHEW 18:12–13

Do you feel like the lamb who strays or one of the
ninety-nine left on the hill? It's always been a little confusing
that the lost sheep would get the more rejoicing, kind of like
the prodigal son who comes home after selfishly squandering
his inheritance while the other son stayed home and worked.
We want justice, equality, or at the very least tidiness. The
justice of God is not our justice, and we must trust that we
are loved in such a way that "equality" is not a measure or
issue or any part of it.

Isaiah 40:1–11
Psalm 96
Matthew 18:12–14

He does not faint nor grow weary.
—ISAIAH 40:28

The image that comes to me is this: I am being hidden,
guarded in a mighty fortress, a castle impenetrable by the
enemy because constantly patrolling the perimeter, ever
alert, never weary, never faint, is an army of angels. They
need no rest; they require no sleep or food. Their eyes see
deep into the horizon; they hear the slightest hint of danger
long before it arrives; they are the perfect sentinels. And
their power comes from their King, my King.

Isaiah 40:25–31
Psalm 103
Matthew 11:28–30

I will help you, says the LORD;
. . . I will make of you a threshing sledge,
sharp, new, and double-edged.
To thresh the mountains and crush them,
to make the hills like chaff.
—ISAIAH 41:14–15

My friend Teresa is a powerful weapon for the Lord. She does not back down from a fight and is not afraid of what the truth requires of us. She doesn't let me forget that I do not know the future; she is willing to help me confront my limitations and my desperate need to sort out heart and soul.

Today we pray for our loved ones who call us to live with greater integrity, and then walk with us through the pain that such growth requires.

Isaiah 41:13–20
Psalm 145
Matthew 11:11–15

DECEMBER 12

• OUR LADY OF GUADALUPE •

Silence, all mankind, in the presence of the LORD! For he stirs forth from his holy dwelling.
—ZECHARIAH 2:17

The regular practice of silence is an essential call that resonates throughout Scripture. We silence ourselves to prepare for prayer, for our hearts to listen and thus be converted. We silence ourselves to prepare for an indwelling of God's presence. We silence ourselves in awe, in holy anticipation, in the reality of our smallness and of God's great love—a love that breaks into human history with miracles and visions, Annunciation, Incarnation, and forgiveness.

Zechariah 2:14–17 or Revelation
11:19a; 12:1–6a, 10ab
Judith 13:18bcde, 19
Luke 1:26–38 or Luke1:39–47

DECEMBER 13

• ST. LUCY, VIRGIN AND MARTYR •

Once again, O LORD of hosts,
look down from heaven, and see;
Take care of this vine,
and protect what your right hand has planted,
the son of man whom you yourself made strong.
—PSALM 80:15–16

One of the great existential needs of the human person is to be seen. Paradoxically, we both desire and fear this reality because what becomes visible is not only our true selves as created by God but also our weakness and sin. The confessional is the perfect meeting of this paradox in that we can maintain a proper privacy without facilitating secrecy.

St. Lucy, patron saint of the eyes, give us clear and holy vision of the Spirit to see ourselves and others and allow them to see us.

Sirach 48:1–4, 9–11
Psalm 80
Matthew 17:9a, 10–13

*He has sent me to bring glad tidings to the poor,
to heal the brokenhearted.*
—ISAIAH 61:1

The question that lingered over her was heavy indeed: what
if he doesn't love me? Or worse, what if he can't? This
brokenhearted healing, these glad tidings, this promise of
relief and wholeness and true communion—all are here now.
Let Jesus reach through the temporal veil and draw you out
of time and into the eternity that already exists in the
sacraments and the intercession of saints and angels and the
faithful departed. In this present eternity, God is healing the
brokenhearted and bringing the message of perfect joy.

Isaiah 61:1–2a, 10–11
Luke 1:46–48, 49–50, 53–54
1 Thessalonians 5:16–24
John 1:6–8, 19–28

DECEMBER 15

Your ways, O LORD, make known to me;
teach me your paths,
Guide me in your truth and teach me,
for you are God my savior.
—PSALM 25:4–5

There is nothing quite so beautiful and quite so convincing as a teachable spirit. I think of a scholar I know who is so deeply invested in finding and living the truth that she would readily change her stance on even the most important issues as more truth was revealed to her. She is not attached to her own ego or pride, the opinions of others, or that savage slave driver, I Need to Be Right.

Numbers 24:2–7, 15–17a
Psalm 25
Matthew 21:23–27

DECEMBER 16

*They shall do no wrong
and speak no lies;
Nor shall there be found in their mouths
a deceitful tongue.*
—ZEPHANIAH 3:13

The Church teaches that "a lie does real violence to another."
Yes, and still my capacity for deception is sometimes truly
astounding. One of the worst versions of this offense is what
I do *not* say when I am afraid to stand up for the truth
because of what someone else might think. To speak no lies
means I will accept the consequences of living in the
truth—punishment, alienation, resentment, or the enduring
anger or misunderstanding of others.

Zephaniah 3:1–2, 9–13
Psalm 34
Matthew 21:28–32

DECEMBER 17

Assemble and listen.
—GENESIS 49:2

We come together to listen, to receive the Advent message,
the promise of the Gospel. One is coming who will save us,
redeem us, and make a way to heaven for us. We receive it as
individuals, yes, but also as a community of persons. There's
great power in stepping out of our solitude, in rejecting the
notion of isolation and entering into the bigger picture,
finding our role in the contours of human history.

Genesis 49:2, 8–10
Psalm 72
Matthew 1:1–17

DECEMBER 18

The angel of the Lord appeared to him in a dream.
—MATTHEW 1:20

This angel offered concrete instruction through a dream. In this season of angels, we are reminded that as Vinita Hampton Wright tells us, "Angels can give revelation to people in dreams and in this way interact with human imagination." A young mother I know consecrates the dreams of her children to heaven's protection every night as she tucks them into bed. Whether angels appear or not, we might all offer our dreams to heaven.

Jeremiah 23:5–8
Psalm 72
Matthew 1:18–25

And the angel of the LORD appeared to the woman and said . . .
—JUDGES 13:3

Our catechism of angelic beings continues. Maria Pia Giudici writes, "Wherever innocence is most oppressed and trampled upon is precisely where the angels are likely to intervene. But also wherever correction or punishment is called for, the angels are likewise apt to be present. . . . They represent the two characteristic faces of the heavens . . . [T]hey are either suffused with sunlight or dark with menacing clouds; in either case the help they send down upon the earth is always beneficial."

Judges 13:2–7, 24–25a
Psalm 71
Luke 1:5–25

DECEMBER 20

The angel Gabriel was sent from God . . . to a virgin
[named] . . . Mary. And coming to her, he said . . .
—LUKE 1:26–27

Are you tempted to imagine that life would be so much
simpler if an angel would simply appear and tell you what's
going to happen and what you're supposed to do? We are
probably better attended, guided, guarded, and ministered to
by angels than we may realize.

Lord, increase my sensitivity to those invisible realities that
help form the way ahead.

Isaiah 7:10–14
Psalm 24
Luke 1:26–38

Sunday

DECEMBER 21

• FOURTH SUNDAY OF ADVENT •

And [the angel Gabriel] coming to her, he said, "Hail, full of grace! The Lord is with you." But she was greatly troubled at what was said and pondered what sort of greeting this might be.
—LUKE 1:28–29

That Mary was troubled at the appearance of the angel with such a greeting is probably great evidence of her innocence and complete lack of presumption. Is this why we seem to hear more stories of angels appearing to children than to adults? Does their innocence leave greater space for miraculous visitations?

2 Samuel 7:1–5, 8b–12, 14a, 16
Psalm 89
Romans 16:25–27
Luke 1:26–38

*"I am the woman who stood near you here, praying to the
LORD. I prayed for this child, and the LORD granted my request.
Now I, in turn, give him to the LORD."*
—1 SAMUEL 1:26–28

Do I give all the gifts of God back to him? Do I consecrate
my work, relationships, talents, and resources to the Lord?
Do I let him do as he will with the gift of my life?

1 Samuel 1:24–28
1 Samuel 2:1, 4–5, 6–7, 8abcd
Luke 1:46–56

All who heard these things took them to heart, saying, "What, then, will this child be? For surely the hand of the Lord was with him."
—LUKE 1:66

There are some among us marked from the beginning for particularly great and terrible tasks. This does not mean, however, that the hand of the Lord is with some of us more or less than with others. God extends his grace in generous, endless amounts to all who will receive it. There is no one who has not been set aside in the heart of God for a particular life, particular gifts and callings.

Malachi 3:1–4, 23–24
Psalm 25
Luke 1:57–66

DECEMBER 24

*In the tender compassion of our God
the dawn from on high shall break upon us,
to shine on those who dwell in darkness and the shadow
of death,
and to guide our feet into the way of peace.*
—LUKE 1:78–79

This is the way we determine the difference between
enabling and compassion. Enabling keeps a person in
darkness and sin; compassion invites the person to step out
of darkness and death and into the light of truth and reality.
Enabling accepts unacceptable behavior without naming it;
compassion, tender and holy, names sin for what it truly is,
and by naming it, confronts it with love.

2 Samuel 7:1–5, 8b–12, 14a, 16
Psalm 89
Luke 1:67–79

Thursday

DECEMBER 25

No more shall people call you "Forsaken,"
or your land "Desolate,"
but you shall be called "My Delight,"
and your land "Espoused."
For the LORD delights in you
and makes your land his spouse.
—ISAIAH 62:4–5

The matrimonial imagery is not merely symbolic, it is sacramental. We are chosen and taken up in union of body and soul with our Beloved. The result of this union is new life, and more than what is possible in isolation.

VIGIL:
Isaiah 62:1–5
Psalm 89
Acts 13:16–17, 22–25
Matthew 1:1–25 or 1:18–25

MIDNIGHT:
Isaiah 9:1–6
Psalm 96
Titus 2:11–14
Luke 2:1–14

DAWN:
Isaiah 62:11–12
Psalm 97
Titus 3:4–7
Luke 2:15–20

DAY:
Isaiah 52:7–10
Psalm 98
Hebrews 1:1–6
John 1:1–18 or 1:1–5, 9–14

Friday

DECEMBER 26

• ST. STEPHEN, FIRST MARTYR •

Be my rock of refuge,
a stronghold to give me safety.
—PSALM 31:3

The North Shore of Lake Superior is a great and terrible
rocky coast, heavy and dark and immovable. The waves
crash and the sun beats down, but wind and weather,
however relentless and powerful, cannot intimidate that
rocky coast. The rocks know their place; they will not yield;
they will not be penetrated; they will not be moved.

Acts 6:8–10; 7:54–59
Psalm 31
Matthew 10:17–22

The life was made visible.
—1 JOHN 1:2

We believe in all things, visible and invisible. And some were made visible. The truth is not an abstraction; the Truth is a person—born, raised, living, crucified, resurrected, and living still.

1 John 1:1–4
Psalm 97
John 20:1a, 2–8

DECEMBER 28

• THE HOLY FAMILY OF JESUS, MARY, AND JOSEPH •

Let the peace of Christ control your hearts, the peace into
which you were also called in one body.
—COLOSSIANS 3:15

A young Catholic man writes to me to say that it's perfectly
normal that newlyweds should spend their first year fighting
viciously. He says he once tried to break down the door on
his young wife. We have become wildly estranged from what
holy family life might be. Such losses of self-control might
be common, but they are hardly normal, hardly a reflection
of the peace of Christ that controls the heart.

Jesus, save our families.

Sirach 3:2–6, 12–14 or Genesis
15:1–6; 21:1–3
Psalm 128
Colossians 3:12–21 or 3:12–17 or
Hebrews 11:8, 11–12, 17–19
Luke 2:22–40 or 2:22, 39–40

"Behold, this child is destined for the fall and rise of many in Israel, and to be a sign that will be contradicted . . . so that the thoughts of many hearts may be revealed."
—LUKE 2:34–35

The revelation of our hearts is a great act of mercy. It is only in revealing the reality of our hearts, naming our sin, identifying our fears, that they may be removed and our hearts may be remade in the image of Christ.

1 John 2:3–11
Psalm 96
Luke 2:22–35

DECEMBER 30

The world and its enticements are passing away.
—1 JOHN 2:17

Note how John defines "the world and its enticements":
sensual lust, enticement for the eyes, and a pretentious life. It
makes sense to love the Great Lakes, to thoroughly enjoy a
beautifully prepared meal you share with your best friends,
to sit in a garden reading a good book, to be moved by a
Bach sonata or the laughter of your grandchildren. We are
sensible—sense-filled—creatures, and we are to find delight
and joy in the world God created—especially in the ways in
which we find more of Him in it.

1 John 2:12–17
Psalm 96
Luke 2:36–40

The LORD comes.
—PSALM 96:13

As John says, the Lord comes to bring his fullness where we receive "grace in place of grace," "grace and truth," "power to become children of God." The Lord comes; he comes for you, to bring you grace, truth, power, and an inheritance as his child. Merry Christmas and Happy New Year. The Lord comes.

1 John 2:18–21
Psalm 96
John 1:1–18

About the Author

Elizabeth M. Kelly is the author of both fiction and nonfiction books, including *The Rosary: A Path into Prayer* (Loyola Press), and a jazz singer who has released two CDs. She currently lives in St. Paul, Minnesota, and is pursuing graduate work in Catholic studies at the University of St. Thomas.

Also by Elizabeth M. Kelly

The Rosary
A Path into Prayer
$11.95 • Pb • 2024-1
Also available as an eBook

The Rosary, full of the history and practice of this great devotion, includes surprising and moving personal testimonies from the author, other devotees, and saints and holy figures, showing how rosary devotion is a practical and gratifying means of meditation that every person can use.

May Crowning, Mass, and Merton
50 Reasons I Love Being Catholic
$13.95 • Pb • 2025-8
Also available as an eBook

Kelly lists 50 reasons to embrace the Catholic faith, such as daily Mass, kneelers in church, and the crucifix. With wit and great affection, covering everything from Michelangelo's creation frescoes to Pope John Paul II, this lay Catholic reminds us all why the Catholic faith is so special.

Continue the Conversation

If you enjoyed this book, then connect with Loyola Press to continue the conversation, engage with other readers, and find out about new and upcoming books from your favorite spiritual writers.

Visit us at **LoyolaPress.com** to create an account and register for our newsletters.

Or click on the code to the left with your smartphone.

Connect with us through:

Facebook
facebook.com
/loyolapress

Twitter
twitter.com
/loyolapress

YouTube
youtube.com
/loyolapress